Evil in ▌

David Thurlow is the aut▌
Norfolk Nightmare and *P.▌* ▌r, all
published by Robert Hale ▌ ▌is own name and
the pseudonym Jonathan Macgowan he has also
written thirteen crime thrillers. He is a journalist.

Evil in
East Anglia

David Thurlow

ROBERT HALE · LONDON

© *David Thurlow 1993*
First published in Great Britain 1993

ISBN 0 7090 5182 4
Robert Hale Limited
Clerkenwell House
Clerkenwell Green
London EC1R 0HT

2 4 6 8 10 9 7 5 3 1

Photoset in Palatino by
Derek Doyle & Associates, Mold, Clwyd.
Printed in Great Britain by
St Edmundsbury Press Ltd, Bury St Edmunds, Suffolk.
Bound by WBC Bookbinders Ltd, Bridgend, Mid-Glamorgan.

Contents

For all old friends in
the police and press who
covered most of these
stories with me

Acknowledgements

I covered many of these cases myself but I am very grateful to Fulton Gillespie, Tom Tarling and my former colleagues in *The Times* library for their expert knowledge and help.

In certain cases, where indicated, the names have been changed to save distress.

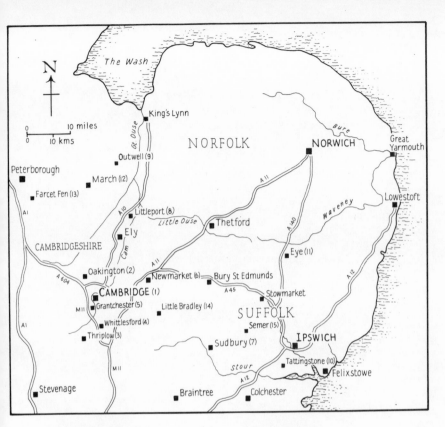

(1) **Cambridge**
The Cambridge rapist
Two football killings
Champagne Charlie

(2) **Oakington**
Gypsy Jack Smith

(3) **Thriplow**
The Greek murderer

(4) **Wittlesford**
Mace-swinging landlord

(5) **Grantchester**
Byron's killing pool

(6) **Newmarket**
Home of Rachel Parsons,
millionaire and racehorse owner

(7) **Sudbury**
American Air Force killing

(8) **Littleport**
Hiding mother

(9) **Outwell**
Killing for the wrong loot

(10) **Tattingstone**
The doctors' hiding place

(11) **Eye**
Eternal triangle

(12) **March**
A different triangle

(13) **Farcet Fen**
Debt leads to murder

(14) **Little Bradley**
Nagging wife dies

(15) **Semer**
Nagging husband

Introduction

If you go east from Cambridge, leaving behind its university and the industrial town that tourists do not see, and take the road to Newmarket, twelve miles away, the countryside is still undulating with a softer green than you find when you reach the headquarters of racing and the split in the counties.

The boundary line runs through the racecourse, and if you go south you are in Suffolk, the part of the county where history abounds – Bury St Edmunds, the old market towns of Lavenham and Sudbury and Hadleigh, places like Long Melford and Clare – until you reach Ipswich and the coast where there is as distinct a change in character as there is between Portsmouth and Southampton in Hampshire.

If you go north you go into the hinterland of Cambridgeshire, once a county of 119 villages and no town, until the administrators took away its individuality and that of the Isle of Ely, Huntingdonshire and the Soke of Peterborough and made it one, a fact still ignored by the older people who like what they had.

Over the border of the old Cambridgeshire lies what was the Isle of Ely, where Hereward warded off his enemies, and home of the Fen Tigers, named after their ancestors' ferocious fighting against the Dutch. These hardy men have had their myths and legends for centuries but exist today as hard working experts at events and work where strength is paramount.

From Newmarket, along the road to Ely, where the cathedral towers into the sky and can be seen for miles, the land drops towards and below sea level. As you travel through Fordham and drop down a few inches to Soham, the countryside changes. The green becomes harsher, the soil blacker and richer, for this is the vegetable garden of England, where the wind howls across from Russia via the North Sea and the flatland of Norfolk.

The natural windbreaks, the trees and the hedges, are long gone, victims of modern husbandry and farming methods. On a fine summer's day the wind can whisk the soil into a whirling spiral high into the blue sky. On a cold winter's day it becomes a desolate landscape, heavy with leaden grey skies and fields of sullen soil.

It has a beauty, stark and gripping, that some delight in. Others huddle by the fire or go west. Those who are there are mainly normal people living their lives as they want to without disrupting the community.

But it is typical of the area that when brutal, evil, wicked crime and violence occurs, it has a distinct flavour of something different.

As a taste we can start in Wicken, just below Soham, a village world-famous for its bird sanctuary. The village, which is split by the back road to Ely or the deep fen through Chatteris (home town of boxing champions Eric Boon and Dave 'Boy' Green) March and Wisbech and out into Norfolk and its history goes back centuries.

At the turn of the century the village had a change of policeman. He was ultra-keen, determined to keep the law to its exact letter and woe betide anyone who infringed it in any way. He ignored the wisdom of the sergeant who told him to let things carry on as usual. For the villagers of Wicken had one night of pleasure a week after six back-breaking days cutting peat out in the fen or toiling over their smallholdings.

On Saturday evenings husbands went down to the Maid's Head to replenish their lost sweat, taking their wives with them. They did not stay late because Sunday morning was church but sometimes closing time (ten o'clock) crept by without anyone noticing.

The new young constable did. He went into the pub dead on ten, roared and shouted that they were breaking the law and if he caught them again he would summons the lot of them.

Some of the older men had a word with the sergeant during the week and he had a word with the village bobby who retorted that if the sergeant suggested just once more that he should turn a blind eye to a deliberate flouting of the law, he would report the sergeant too.

The next Saturday the pub was packed and everyone forgot the warning of the week before until – through the fug and smoke – came the caped constable with his notebook ready. He took every name and as the villagers trudged miserably out, they knew they would have to appear in court. The landlord closed up with a heavy heart. It would mean the end of his licence.

On the Tuesday, as the bobby sat in his little office writing out the summonses, one of the village elders came to tell him that someone had opened the gate of the horse pound on the green and the horses were out on the fen.

It was nearing dusk and already the soft mist that rises like a blanket, hovering a few inches off the ground, could be seen against the brilliant background of the winter sun going down.

The constable knew his duty and went off onto the fen to round the horses up. In the distance he could see a light, a fire burning. The fen can be a lonely place and if you did not know it you could be in trouble. You could be in trouble even if you did.

Dusk is like a quilt on the fen, aided by the fog drawn up by the dampness of the soil. But there was a light ahead and the constable carried on ....

By night he had not returned. The horses had come home like pigeons for their food. The next morning the

worried sergeant led a reluctant search party, going only
because as much as they disliked him, they did not want
him to have come to any harm.

But he had. He was lying by a dead bonfire with head
injuries. The fire had been the siren to lure him out there.

Back in the village it was found that the summonses the
policeman had been so busy writing had gone – and so
had two Tigers, strapping lads. No one was certain that
the constable had been killed unlawfully because it might
have been during a fight but the men were gone and were
never heard of again.

The First World War went by and Tigers were
slaughtered in the mud of France and Belgium. In the
second war Tigers were in the Cambridgeshires who went
into the bag with the Suffolks and the Norfolks at
Singapore (many had never been further than their county
towns) and many died on the Burma Railway. For every
sleeper laid a man died, and even now the still of summer
nights can be torn by the screams of a former Japanese
prisoner, nightmaring the horrors in his voice.

The war was well over when the doctor was called to an
old woman who was dying in the village.

She asked the doctor to do her a favour. From under her
pillow she pulled a crumpled envelope, with an American
postmark over its American stamps, posted to her at Ely
Post Office at the turn of the century.

It was from her son, one of the two Tigers who had fled
after the death of the policeman. It said that he and his
friend had reached America and were all right.

The old lady could not read but her instinct told her that
it was from her son when it finally arrived at the Post
Office which again by instinct, she knew some form of
communication addressed to her would. How many times
she went to the Post Office, asking if there was a letter for
her, no one knows.

But she died happy.

This is a typical crime of the area. Like Suffolk, the

murders and violence have a whiff of the bizarre, the unusual, about them. The crimes do not occur regularly because the region is too thinly populated or perhaps people are less criminally inclined.

But when they do crop up they encompass strange and weird human behaviour.

Let us start with Suffolk. It may not have the reputation of Norfolk to murdering outsiders as a place in which to dump bodies but in 1967 two suitcases were found in a field at Tattingstone, just off the A12 London to Ipswich road and not far from the county town.

In the cases were the pieces that once were a sixteen-year-old boy, who had been assaulted, strangled and then cut expertly by a person with medical and surgical experience. The inquiry led police into a twilight world both on the Shotley peninsula and in north London.

Down the road in the Crown Court at Ipswich, two strange tales of naggers and manslaughter have been told in recent years. The first involved a young married man who said his wife had gone off with her American boyfriend based at the huge Wethersfield base near their home. She had not.

Then there was a woman church warden, twice his age, who stood in the same dock charged with killing her farmer husband over who should cut the lawn. That of course was not the real reason, just the fuse to cause it.

It was in the old assizes court at Bury St Edmunds that the former Lord Chancellor and Attorney General, the late Lord Havers, then plain Michael, who figures in several of these crimes, defended an American mother, thousands of miles from home in a strange country, who had stabbed her serviceman husband on a Sunday afternoon. He never needed to die and when he did the Americans snatched his body before the defence could send their own pathologist to do a post mortem.

But it was in Newmarket that two of Suffolk's oddest cases took place; the servant who killed because he was not paid, and the ex-lover who believed he had been wronged in the everlasting eternal triangle.

The servant was a stable lad who killed one of the richest and most eccentric women in Britain, brilliant and almost a genius before her time, who degenerated into a foul-mouthed mean old hag. Her background took her onto the front pages of the world.

Many years later, not far down the road in racing's headquarters, a gun dealer drove over one hundred miles to confront the beautician who had chosen another man, a local auctioneer. Armed and ready to shoot the girl, it did not happen as he had planned, and he pumped bullets into his rival as if he was finishing off game.

Back in Cambridgeshire and at the north of the county where it borders with Norfolk, three Tigers heard tales of wealth at a farm just ouside Wisbech, a town brimming with character, fine houses and the birthplace of Thomas Clarkson, the anti-slavery campaigner. In the pubs it was whispered that the farmer had untold fortunes in his safe. The Tigers went there with enough rope to tie up a ship. Their information was wrong. The farmer had a fortune but it was not in the safe. That held just 20p.

Just down the road in March, Wisbech's great rival as capital of the Fens, newcomers were involved in an offbeat crime of passion. A school teacher took a knife to his wife in desperation and threw her lover through the plate glass front door. Her lover was another woman and this was ten years before lesbian love became common.

March was the home town of a man, born evil, whose life of crime could never be cured. He was in trouble from the very start, stealing, housebreaking, crime after crime, and spent most of his time in approved schools or Borstal and undergoing corrective training, penal servitude and preventitive detention. He came from a very respectable family but before he was ten a local policeman forecast that he would eventually hang for murder. He was wrong about hanging because it had been abolished by the time the man did kill but he did murder his lover by strangling her with a stocking and tossing her body into the sea.

Across the bleak fen from March, just a bit further north, a man whose small lorry company was in terrible straits went out late at night to kill the source of money he knew was there for the taking. He used the same local knowledge to get rid of the owner and his body.

Back to the city of learning and the area around Cambridge.

It was never renowned for its part in the shameful history of football violence although it had its low key share. It did however have two killings directly connected with the game and a fan was jailed for five years for kicking a policeman in the head while he was being held by other youths.

The two killings were not at the ground. The first involved an eleven-year-old boy who cheeked a sixteen-year-old waitress during the game in the way that boys of that age sometimes do. She chased him on the common land afterwards and caught him.

She drowned him as he pleaded with her not to kill him. He was not to know that she was mentally ill.

The other killer had no excuse although he was contrite afterwards. He was out on bail and roaming the range with friends in a car when they spotted some Wolverhampton Wanderers' fans on their way home from a match at Ipswich, who had stopped in Cambridge for refreshment. In those days there was no by-pass so their route went through the city.

The fan, the same age as the waitress, was armed with a brick and as the car passed the Wolves' fans he lent out of the car window as far as he could and hurled it.

It struck a sales rep, aged twenty-one, and he went down like a log, dead.

Just outside Cambridge, at Byron's Pool where the poet used to go, another innocent man died just because he was there. Mr S. was an angler and a member of the

League Against Cruel Sports. He met a man shooting birds who shot him as well.

Equally ruthless was the murder of a sub-post mistress in the village of Thriplow. The killer was a Greek who took his lover in a clapped-out caravanette and dropped off their children with babysitters on the way to the terrible crime. Police used trickery of the highest order to catch him.

And even worse, if it can be, was the slaughter of a mother as she cycled home across the fields near Oakington on the other side of Cambridge and met a modern brigand out with his gun and bandolier. As is the case in all these accounts he introduced the extra element which takes his appalling crime out of the ordinary.

Perhaps the strangest murder was the story of the brooding farm labourer in Eye, Suffolk, who fell for his friend's wife – 'I picked her up like a painted doll. I thought I had got a rare capture.'

The smouldering passions in the fields led to carnage, with the killer turning the gun onto the wrong side of his chest, failing to kill himself.

Then there are those crimes which didn't involve death, but were equally as bizarre or horrific:

The landlord of one of the most popular out-of-town pubs in Cambridgeshire took a mace and halberd from the wall when an argument over a barefooted girl developed into a bloody battle. He was host to generations of undergraduates but his actions that night nearly took him away from his bar into a prison cell. He was fined instead.

In Cambridge itself were two men, both habitual criminals, both quite different.

One was Champagne Charlie who lived high on other people's money and champagne when out of prison. He met a wealthy Cambridge widow and took her for thousands, bigamously married her and even had her practising curtsies for the Royal Ball when she would meet the Queen during Ascot week. He turned to violence when she rejected him and he tried to win her back.

The other was a professional, lifelong housebreaker who went to rob in Cambridge bedsit land and stayed to rape. Over several months as the Cambridge rapist he became internationally notorious and his attacks became more and more vicious. He created terror amongst thousands of girls who lived on their own. He was sent to prison for life and the judge said that in his case it should mean life.

The last story is of a former officer with the Palestine police who returned to the fens a changed man. When his mother died he could not accept the fact and concealed the body for eleven years (but still collecting her pension money) until he was caught.

He may have looked a recluse but when police made enquiries they found that he was worth over £400,000 in shares and savings.

When he appeared in the dock at King's Lynn Crown Court, the prosecutor said, 'It is said there are many strange stories about the Fens. This is one of the strangest of all.'

If he had included Suffolk in the strange stories he would have been right.

You have had a taste. Now read the details.

1   Football

Two Killings by Young Fans

To the visitor, the city of Cambridge is the university. Internationally, Cambridge is a city of learning, a place of beautiful buildings and beautiful people, young people racing from lecture room to sports field, debating at the union, performing in the footlights or in a college play, studying in the library, rowing or punting on the river, going to parties, or dancing the night away at May balls. King's Parade, Trinity Street, Magdalen Street, the Senate House, the colleges, the sports grounds, Fenners, Grange Road – these are names that the people who flock by the hundred thousand annually know and love. It is the photographs, etchings, paintings and postcards of these places that they take away.

But the truth is quite different. The university is only a small part of the city. The rest is an industrial town and it is separate, giving a town and gown situation, two compartments apart. In the old days there used to be a town v. gown atmosphere and occasionally trouble. Not now. The two stay in their own compounds. The real Cambridge is by far the largest town in the county and the fens although there are many who would argue that it should not be classed as fen even though it stands on the edge of the sweep of bare landscape that stretches as far as the eye can see and where sound on a crisp night travels even further.

One night, the late and great Tommy Cooper was guest at a staff dinner at the company who run the airport business, and when he came out he found that he had a puncture. His marvellous laugh that entertained millions could be heard (they swore) in a village fifteen miles away as it cracked through the stillness of a bitter moonlit night.

As well as the airport, there are television, computer, microchip, motor building and service companies, employing thousands. There are sweeping avenues of fine houses, private and council estates and some tight areas of mean houses and poverty. It is a mix and the east side is not so prosperous (but by no means poor) as the west.

The football ground, home of Cambridge United, is on the road out to the east, Newmarket and Norfolk and Suffolk.

The team had a small but faithful following in the late 60s and the 70s. I used to take my son and his friend regularly and there was never any trouble. No one imagined there would be and no one gave it a thought. The stadium was windswept and no one could call the seating comfortable, but it was adequate and the spectators were people used to biting winds and the cold.

It was therefore a shock when one of the young fans, just a boy of eleven, was murdered after an evening match in April 1967. The second killing involving Cambridge United and a rival team occurred ten years later when football hooliganism was the plague sweeping the sport. That two such things should happen in Cambridge is typical of the way violence erupts in the area. Neither happened at the football ground and was nothing to do with the club.

The murder in 1967 occurred because the eleven-year-old boy, John (not his real name) was with some friends, and as boys do, were running about at half time and spotted a sixteen-year-old girl whom they knew and used to tease by calling her names. The girl, a waitress, shouted back. She did not like the insults but she always gave as good as she got. She had caught one of his friends once before and hit him but John had given her the slip.

The game ended and on the way out the boy in a daring mood, ran up to the girl, called her a name and ran off. He was just a little boy being cocky and cheeky and thinking it great fun.

He had absolutely no idea that he was baiting a psychopathic killer.

He followed the girl on her way home, not far from the ground, still larking about (as he thought). She was burning with anger and longing to get her hands on him. Near some garages by her home she suddenly turned and grabbed him.

She told the police later what happened and her statement was read out when she appeared at Cambridgeshire Assizes in Cambridge two months later.

She said: 'I grabbed him and dragged him across the common. He was struggling and shouting. I pushed him into the river and we struggled.'

The river was a small brook that ran across Coldham's Common, not far from their homes.

She went on telling what happened in what was a full confession to Chief Inspector Christine Willis in the early hours of the morning after her arrest. A bed was made up in the Chief Inspector's room at 2.40 a.m. but the waitress could not sleep and wanted to talk. She went on to tell the senior policewoman what occurred after she had pushed John into the brook.

'He tried to get out but I caught hold of his leg and he pushed me in. He got out and I did and I got my lanyard round his neck and pulled it. I had a knife on my lanyard in a sheath. I said I was going to kill him.'

The girl was very matter-of-fact for reasons we will come to. Imagine the scene: the girl in her made-up bed, the woman police officer sitting in her chair, writing down what the girl – who had been cautioned that she need not say anything but continued to chatter on – was saying. No doubt there were cups of tea about.

What the girl said next was quite disturbing.

'He started praying,' she said. Picture this petrified little boy, soaking wet, with this girl he had tormented, bigger than him, taking her lanyard and preparing to kill him. No wonder he prayed.

The girl went on: 'Poor kid, it didn't do him any good though, did it?'

But it was not quite as it appeared.

Chief Inspector Willis asked, 'When was he praying – before or after he went into the river?'

'Before. I had my knife out and as we went in the river I pushed it in the back pocket of my jeans. When we were out of the water I felt for it in the sheath but it wasn't there. It must have fallen in the water.'

The policewoman considered what she had been told. Then she asked the question anyone would have asked.

'I suppose you are sorry now?'

The girl did not answer so the policewoman tried again. 'Why did you do this to him?'

'Who?'

'The boy who died tonight.'

'I can't stand little kids getting in my way. I'd still do it again if he got in my way, to anyone who would get in my way.'

Then the girl went to sleep but was woken by police cars and men arriving in the yard outside the office. She went on telling Chief Inspector Willis about it.

It was a casual opening remark as if what she had done was of little importance.

'I can't understand what all the fuss is about. When I left him his head was in the water but before that he was alive, at least I think he was.'

'How do you know that?'

'I was leaning over him, wasn't I? His heart was still beating.'

'Why didn't you leave him like that?'

The girl did not hesitate. 'Well I couldn't leave him alive, could I, let's face it, so I shoved his face in the water.'

What happened after that was revealed at both the committal proceedings – for in those days all the evidence was given in public at the lower magistrates court to prove there was a prima facie case to go for trial instead of a bundle of documents and statements being handed in as now – at Cambridge and then in the Assize court.

The girl, soaked from the waist down, left John in the brook and headed home. On her way home she telephoned the lady who was in charge of the youth organization to which she belonged and asked her, 'Can I talk to you? I have just killed a child.' She said she was in a phone box not far away and the commandant of the group, driven by her husband, hurried round there. The girl was standing on the other side of the road and when the woman called to her she ignored her as if not recognizing her.

A little while later the girl arrived home with her father. She had not spoken on the way but when she reached home everyone noticed that she was soaking wet from the waist down. Eventually she told her father that she had strangled a boy with a piece of string down at the brook and added, 'I left him lying in the ditch by the garages.'

When the police arrived, called by the distraught parents of the girl, for they did not really know what had happened, the girl was asked how she had got wet. She said that she and the boy had had a fight and she had strangled him.

The boy's parents were then told and their heartbreak began, never to end.

The girl and the piece of string, the lanyard she treasured, were taken to the police station and it was during that night that she told Chief Inspector Willis all about it.

It is, sadly, an example of how slowly the wheels of justice turn now, in that the girl was tried in Cambridge less than two months after her terrible crime. Nowadays it would be at least six months, probably a year before she would appear. In the time between her committal for trial from the juvenile court and the assizes she was examined by several doctors including the medical officer at Holloway prison for women.

All agreed that she was mentally ill.

So when she appeared in the dock and pleaded guilty to killing John due to diminished responsibility but not guilty of murder, her pleas were accepted by the prosecution.

Dr Norman Mullin from Holloway prison said: 'I have come to the conclusion that she is suffering from a psychopathic disorder within the meaning of the Mental Health Act 1959 and I consider she is in need of treatment. In my opinion it was substantially impairing her mental responsibility and this is the unanimous view of three doctors.'

He added that Broadmoor hospital could take the girl for treatment immediately.

Mr Michael Havers, QC, prosecuting, said: 'The girl, after some minor argument with the boy, strangled him and left him with his head lying in a river and he eventually died. She has been examined by several doctors and it is quite clear that she is mentally ill.'

And although he did not stress it, it was also quite clear that John was dead and no form of treatment would have brought him round. It was just his misfortune that he should meet someone out of their mind.

The defence had their little say too. Mr Hugh Griffiths, QC, said: 'This is a tragic case. The girl has been examined on behalf of the defence by an independent doctor and he has come to agreement with the findings of the other doctors. Both the girl and her parents appreciate that she is in need of treatment.'

The judge, Mr Justice Glyn-Jones, had the final say.

'This case needs few words from me. All the medical evidence leaves only one course open to me, that is to make a hospital order which means that doctors will have to consult the Home Secretary before acting on the conclusion that you can be safely released, if and when you get better.

'There is every hope that you will get better. Broadmoor is a hospital best suited for your treatment and you will go there straight away.'

He had a word for both sets of parents. 'I realize how terribly distressed they must have been about all this.'

They were, they were. But there was a difference. The killer's parents still had a daughter, albeit a mentally ill one, but so young that cure was almost certain. The victim's parents had lost a son, one of their three children, and he could never be replaced.

What are the chances of a small boy, following the eternal pursuit of teasing a girl, being chased as he probably expected, enjoying the game, probably being prepared to accept a clout if caught, but instead being pushed face down in a brook and then praying on the bank for his life while he is strangled?

About the same chance, I imagine, as those of a man having a drink and a bite to eat outside a pub early on a January evening being killed by a flying brick, hurled at him by a Cambridge United Supporter because he happened to be a football fan.

The irony of it was that the victim, George Brown (not his real name) was supporting Wolverhampton Wanderers, who had been playing at Ipswich, fifty miles away. The only reason he was in Cambridge was because the coach back to the Midlands had stopped on Newmarket Road so the supporters could have some refreshment.

As they stood in the sunshine, a car load of Cambridge supporters drove up and down the road at high speed shouting insults and waving fists. They had been to a Cambridge match and were looking for trouble as fans were any Saturday in the late seventies. This was 1977.

To add to the picture; the potential killer had just been to the police station to report as part of a bail condition.

Once that chore had been completed, the sixteen-year-old, in complete control of his faculties, was ready for trouble.

What happened was told by the prosecutor when he appeared at Norwich crown court (cases are sent to courts where the red judges sit to try murders and serious crimes on the circuit they travel) to admit manslaughter but deny murder, a plea which was accepted.

John Archer, QC, said that the dead man, aged twenty-one and a sales rep from Dudley, was having a drink when it happened.

The Wolves fans were a happy, content group on an enjoyable day out. The Cambridge youths were searching for trouble.

'The defendant was a Cambridge supporter and had been to a Cambridge match with his companions. They were travelling about in two cars, shouting insults at groups of Wolves supporters. The defendant was in a belligerent mood and they had followed a minibus and grabbed a trailing scarf and thrown an aerosol spray out of the car at the coach. Eventually they stopped and he took part of a brick back to the car. As the car drove past at more than 40 mph there was a group of Wolverhampton supporters outside a public house in Newmarket Road. He levered himself out of the window of the car and sitting partly out of the window he threw the brick at the group. The brick struck the victim at the base of the skull behind the left ear and he died.'

Just like that! It was an injury rare in the medical world and unique at that time in the experience of consultant pathologist Professor Austin Gresham. When the inquest was held four months before the trial in June he said:

'The external injury was a large bruise on the upper left side of the neck. This is a very unusual injury, unique in my experience and not very well recorded. Otherwise he was a normal healthy young man. It must have been caused by a blunt, rough object, travelling with considerable kinetic energy because of the intense local damage to the neck muscle and the acute extension of the neck being thrown backwards.'

The force of the blow, by a blunt and rough object – a piece of brick being hurled from a car travelling at 40 mph by a strong young man – had damaged the spinal column and the victim had died almost immediately.

He went down dead to the astonishment, horror and fear of the other fifty from the coach who were around him. One moment he was a fit, healthy, happy young man, the next a corpse ready for the mortuary slab, another football casualty.

The police quickly found the thrower and that was why he was in the dock listening to the prosecutor who then read out his statement.

The youth said, 'We went past some old boys and they started throwing things at us and I threw the brick and he went down.'

There was no evidence that anyone from the coach threw anything at the Cambridge youths. But, Mr Archer said, from what witnesses had said, the Cambridge crowd, the home fans on their own territory, had gone out with the intention of bricking the coach even though they had not been playing Wolves and unless they drew them in the cup were never likely to.

To his credit, the sixteen-year-old killer admitted it. He did not try to shift blame or escape the consequences of what he had done.

His acceptance was given to the judge, Mr Justice Gibson, by John Blofeld, QC, now a High Court judge and brother of Henry Blofeld, the cricket commentator.

He said, 'Everyone must recognize that football violence is an appalling phenomenon and only too prevalent, and courts have a duty to deal with it severely as it can lead to appalling incidents. He recognizes this and nothing I can say can detract from the very seriousness of it.'

'He is appalled at what he has done. He never paused to think that by throwing this brick he might kill someone. '

It was true. He hurled the brick with all his might and never thought of the consequences.

The judge weighed him off for three years, the place of detention to be decided by the Home Secretary. Mr Justice Gibson used the only words that can really be said on such an occasion:

'You killed that young man with a brick. This is a grave offence and you, and others like you must know that the court will deal with such conduct and punish severely.'

Three years is a long time for anyone and even more so for a boy of sixteen. He went off to serve his punishment but it would not deter others. No football hooligan ever hesitates in his tracks as he kicks, maims or punches to think 'what will the judge do if I am caught?'

2 Smith

The Gypsy Who Swung from the Trees to Murder and Rape

In the days before Beeching, a train ran several times a day from Cambridge to March and back, setting off thirty miles to the east of Cambridge and going through the fens calling at places like Wimblington, Chatteris, Somersham and St Ives, and then on across the flat land and fields to Oakington, Histon and Cambridge. It took an hour and was part of the network of buses and trains that linked the 119 villages of the county and the villages and small towns of the Isle of Ely – for you could go on from March to Wisbech and Kings Lynn to the coast at Hunstanton – with Cambridge until the government decided that the people no longer needed it.

It was at Oakington, wartime home of a bomber base from where raid after raid set off for Germany, that Mrs Ethel Cook (not her real name) caught the train every working day to go to Histon to work at Chivers, the jam factory. Many women in the area worked there. Mrs Cook was forty-five and the wife of a civilian batman at the Royal Air Force station for it was then being used as a training school. She would cycle along a bridle path to the station, leave her cycle there, go to work and then return the same way.

July in 1960 was a beautiful month. The sun beat down on the fields as the corn began to ripen and there was a

31

feeling of well-being in the air.

Mrs Cook was riding home without a care in the world along a popular path, at a time in our history when women did ride along on their own without fear. If anything did happen to women it was so rare that it made big headlines.

She was one of the unfortunate ones, one that did make national news.

For unknown to her, a young man who rejoiced in the name of Gypsy Jack Smith, although his real name was William, was out on the prowl with his gun and a bandolier full of cartridges.

As she cycled he was waiting up a tree and when she neared him he swung down like Tarzan and blocked her path.

In one instance the brightness of her day turned into darkness.

What happened next the police could only in the end surmise, but there were plenty of clues to help them make up the picture.

Smith obviously demanded money and then she must have recognized him. Whatever was said is guess work but following the exchange she must have been so terrified that she turned and fled, to escape this man with his gun pointed at her.

She raced into the barley field, hoping and praying, that he would leave her alone, that he would take her bag and money and go.

He did not. Smith, five feet six inches tall with grey eyes and dark hair dyed blonde, went after her. He had a reputation for wildness, for dare-devilry, for petty theft, for being handy with a gun.

Into the field ran the woman, no doubt fighting for breath, screaming for someone to help her.

There was no one else around and her cries were lost in the stillness of the early evening.

Smith raised his gun and fired, shooting Mrs Cook in

the back. She fell in a crumpled heap. It must have been like the scene so beloved by Hollywood film producers where the victim runs for his or her life and the man with the gun waits and then carefully takes aim at the fleeing figure, slowly pulls the trigger and the victim, in full flight, is caught in the back and goes down. In films they tend to stay down, perhaps twitch, but it is over. The bullet does it in one.

But this was not in glorious technicolour in California. This was in a barley field in rural England where one expects to find rabbits and hares and if there is any gunfire it is to kill one of those.

Mrs Cook lay on the ground, badly wounded by the shot from his 12 bore. But instead of leaving her where she was to be found, possibly to be saved, Gypsy Jack swaggered over and stood looking down on her.

In her fear, her justifiable mortal fear, she put her arm over her face to protect herself. Perhaps she begged him not to do it. It made no difference. He blasted the second barrel straight into her.

And as if that was not enough thinking she might be still alive, he turned her over and battered her head with the butt of the gun.

And as if that was not even enough, Gypsy Jack, the big hero, committed a final disgusting horror.

Then, no doubt pleased with himself, he walked away to leave her there.

With him he took her shoes and handbag and the rewards of his robbery and murder: a pound note and eight old pennies (£1.04).

Her body was found soon after. It was the cycle lying under the tree that attracted the attention of a man and woman passing by. They looked across because there appeared to be some kind of trail into the barley field and there they saw the body which was partly clad.

The police were called and the murder inquiry began. Cambridge still had its own police force, and Det

Inspector Percy Fouracre headed the hunt for the killer. It was the practice then for the local force to try and find the murderer but if after a reasonably short time it was obvious that more help was needed they called in Scotland Yard and one of the duty Detective Superintendents would travel out into the provinces accompanied by a sergeant and the famous black murder bag. The man who came to Cambridge was John du Rose, one of the big names from the Yard, who struck apprehension into the hearts of the most hardened London villain.

By the time he arrived, the local team had done a lot of hard work to lay out before the London men, the background and facts of the case. They knew who the victim was, why she was there, what was missing, who the local men were who might or could have been responsible. By elimination it was but a handful. They had also done the house to house enquiries at both ends of the bridle path and in the surrounding villages, and although a man with a gun was a common sight as they hunted rabbits, pigeons and vermin, a man playing around with a gun as if he is showing off or is irresponsible is soon noticed.

Gypsy Jack was one of those who had been noticed. He had been seen at a bus stop – with his gun and a bandolier of cartridges like a Mexican bandit.

The trouble was that he had then disappeared.

More inquiries showed that he lived with his mother Violet who had a ramshackle home built onto the side of an old railway carriage. He had not been home and a watch was kept on the structure, more like a greenhouse than anything else. Sixty men joined the search with a dozen dogs for as the hours passed it was obvious that Gypsy Jack was the man the police wanted. Everything pointed to him and the police issued his name and description which was a rare thing to do. The case had the ingredient, difficult to define but something that all good reporters could sniff like tracker dogs, that makes a good story for the national papers as well as the locals. Local radio did not exist and local television was in its infancy. The national papers came down in force.

The weekend came and still there was no sign of the gypsy. There had been vague sightings in the area in which he was known, by the police, to sleep rough when the fancy took him. What they did not know was that a fifteen-year-old local boy Michael was befriending the killer.

Later he was to tell how Smith asked him to get him some cigarettes and cartridges for his shotgun. The boy had come across him in the fields. He did as he was asked and saw Smith again the next day.

This time Smith talked abut the murder and said, 'I have killed a woman', but did not tell him why and the boy did not ask. Smith said that he still had her handbag and shoes and they were hidden behind a tree. Then he said that he did it because she had put him inside before (which was not true).

He asked for more cartridges but the boy did not get them for him.

On Sunday, Det Superintendent John du Rose and Inspector Percy Fouracre were still baffled. They could not understand where Smith had gone. They knew he was a roamer but in the way a cat roams, inside and along the boundaries of his own territory.

The territory was covered with policemen and their dogs looking for him, with the local public who were as anxious as the police to find the killer. They were worried that if he had done it once he would do it again and would not hesitate should he be cornered. They were joined by people all over the country who had been alerted to the story through the newspapers.

But there was no sign of Smith. He had disappeared. Gypsy camps in the area, the county, all over the country were checked. He had not been to any of those and he would not have been helped. He was a wicked killer of a defenceless woman and no one wanted to know him. Poachers, petty thieves, truants were one thing. Ruthless murderers were quite another and they wanted him found too.

The search went on and the detectives went back to see Smith's mother. She had not seen him. No one in the family knew where he was. They were sure it was not him – that he would not do such a thing.

The detectives talked in the living-room in Mrs Smith's home and then went out into the sunshine.

It was then that they cracked it. They noticed that the lean-to was much smaller inside than it appeared outside. They had a look round and it was obvious that this was indeed the case. The living-room was two or three, perhaps even four feet shorter, than it should have been.

Detecive Superintendent Du Rose and Detective Inspector Fouracre went back inside to confirm their theory.

They were right.

At the end of the small living-room there was an old partition, borded up, and covered by a chest of drawers. There was no conversation with Mrs Smith who stood watching.

Du Rose pulled away the chest of drawers and then began to pull at the boarding. It was old wood and loose and came away easily.

He poked his head in and there was Gypsy Jack sitting nursing his shotgun.

Before Du Rose said a word the killer acted.

He shot himself in the head.

There was no pause, no time to speak to him. Rather than be captured and branded publicly as a wicked killer the gypsy took the quick way out.

Still full of life he perhaps realized that there was nothing in the future but prison and disgrace, and that death was better than that.

The moment must have been horrific for the senior

detective. It does happen. Not far from Oakington, in another fen village, the publican of the local pub suddenly disappeared just before the Christmas Club fund was to be paid out – money that the regulars had collected week by week during the year. There was a tidy sum for everyone. But, as happens every Christmas somewhere in the country, the kitty was bare and the man who ran the club knew that he was caught – in the old criminal parlance – bang to rights. Instead of standing behind the bar to tell his customers that the money had gone he vanished. Or so everyone thought. The local bobby got into the locked pub with a colleague to have a look, to see if the publican had left a clue as to where he might have gone. Upstairs in the bedroom he noticed that there was a door into a cupboard area and that the chest of drawers had been moved and not pulled correctly back into place.

He moved them and opened the door. It was not a cupboard but a storage room and in the centre of the room, caught in the light of the constable's torch, was the landlord.

He was holding a shotgun, the butt between his feet, the barrel under his chin.

The constable was about to say 'now don't be silly' or 'wait a minute, there's no need for that' or some other form of wording to stop the landlord from death for although it was a fairly serious crime and the regulars were very angry, it was not a reason for suicide.

The landlord did not listen, did not hesitate. He blew his head off.

The constable was sick on the spot. Detective Superintendent Du Rose may have felt the same. It certainly came as a terrible shock.

It was the end of the case. The forensic laboratory scientists tested the gun and compared all the evidence they had of the shooting to make absolutely sure that it was Smith's gun that killed Mrs Cook. It was. Her property was recovered and it was proved by fingerprints that it was Smith who had taken it.

He was buried with gypsies coming from miles around for the funeral. An inquest was held.

It was a quick affair. There was not much to be said any more: the killer was dead by his own hand.

The final sting, that put this crime into a different category, came at the very end.

Du Rose told how Smith approached the woman cycling home, how he robbed and threatened her, how no one could say exactly what was said and done that made her run for the barley field.

Du Rose said, in a matter-of-fact way so that the words could be heard but not translated into graphic horror, 'She ran for her life towards the barley field. She was forty-five yards into the field when he shot her. She fell in a crumpled heap and put her arm up to protect her face and he shot her again. And believing she was still alive he then struck her a blow with the butt of the gun.'

And finally the worst statement of all:

'Today I have received a report from New Scotland Yard and it is evident that he then raped her.'

It is no wonder that Smith shot himself rather than listen to that from the dock.

3 Farmakopoulos

The Greek Who Killed for Money

George Farmakopoulos was the kind of Greek that lonely women might fall for. He was handsome and bearded, his skin sunkissed and he had charm and the ability to whisper sweet nothings over food and wine. Some of his relationships were short, others were of a more permanent nature like the one he was enjoying with Maureen. She was a year older and infatuated with George, who dominated her with his vital personality and loving. She had a daughter by him and they lived as man and wife, both in Cambridge and in Greece.

They were apart at this time for a short period but were coming together for a reunion in Amsterdam.

That's why George was ringing the hotel in Amsterdam where Maureen was. George was still in Athens and from a cafe on a wonderful afternoon with the sun beating down, he made the call. No, said the receptionist, it was right that she was there but she could not come to the phone because she was feeding the baby. She would ring back in just a few minutes.

She did. But George had some bad news. He would not now be able to meet her in Amsterdam where they had stayed before, but had decided that he would go to Antwerp and would meet her there the next day. Maureen protested that she did not want to travel with the baby again but George was adamant. Antwerp it must be.

Maureen agreed and put the phone down.

The man by her side nodded and thanked her. Then he went into his office and made some urgent telephone calls to colleagues in Amsterdam and Antwerp.

He was a senior detective in Cambridge and Maureen, aged thirty-nine, mother of two young children and a drug taker, was in custody facing a charge of murder.

She had been arrested when she returned with her children to England after fleeing to Greece with George, aged thirty-eight, and known to Interpol under different names all over Europe where he had a long history of minor crime, after the killing.

She was now being used as the bait to lure her lover back to England. While he thought she was ringing from Amsterdam, she was in the cells. When he rang her mother's house in Stapleford, a village just outside Cambridge, she was hurried there in a police car.

The question was, would George, the braggart who liked to tell tales that put him in a fantasy world of rich living when he did not have a bean, fall for it?

It began in October, 1984, on a rainy afternoon. George and Maureen were over visiting her mother to show her the baby. Her lover was given a frosty reception for his mistress was married and they had come together because Maureen's husband met George in prison. The husband was serving a sentence for drug smuggling. When George came out he went to see Maureen and charmed her. They set up home together and finally arrived in England.

The trouble was that for all his talk the swarthy Greek was broke. He was obsessed with getting money and like so many before and after him, decided that his best bet was a sub post office.

He only decided on the morning of the crime that he would go ahead, after talking about it for a fortnight. His chosen target was at Thriplow, one of the dozens of Cambridgeshire villages.

They set off after lunch with the children and dropped

them off with friends who were acting as babysitters for the robbers.

Maureen explained why she was there when the couple appeared at Norwich crown court many months later.

'I kept saying I was not going to do it and then eventually I just gave in to his constant nagging. He had been nagging me for so long about robbing a post office I just gave in. I was fed up with hearing about it everyday.'

Just like a husband who is nagged about repairing a hinge or painting the bedroom. Nag, nag, nag and off you go and rob a bank.

They arrived in the pouring rain outside the little post office in the attractive village and parked the caravanette. It was their only form of transport and also where the Greek had to sleep. His lover's mother would not let him sleep in the house.

They got out and walked into the shop where Mrs Doreen Smith, aged 53 and widowed, was serving. Maureen's job was to distract her.

Suddenly her lover appeared behind the counter and in his hand was a gun, pointing at Mrs Smith.

The whole operation changed. Maureen knew that George had a gun, but had no idea that he had brought it with him. She had gone to steal some money. No one had mentioned guns.

She was petrified but not nearly as much as the popular sub postmistress who was handed a bag and told to fill it with money from the till by the woman robber.

Maureen told what happened next from the witness box at Norwich. It was a grim tale.

'He was holding a gun with two hands and he pointed it towards her and said "Where is the money? give me the money". I thought he was just going to scare the woman. I never ever thought he would actually use it.'

She was so wrong.

He did fire it although she said that she did not hear the shots or see him do it.

What she did hear as she stepped back out of sight was a mixture of cries and pleas from Mrs Smith. She heard her say 'No, don't' and George order her to 'Get in here' which was a cupboard into which he was pushing the postmistress.

Then Maureen heard her say 'No, don't' again and then what she thought was the sound of a door shutting.

She went on with her story to the jury. 'George came into the shop part of the post office and said "Let's go". I didn't hear any shots.

'When we were driving back to Stapleford he said he had shot her four times.'

Such a normal statement to make I suppose, when you go out robbing and on your way home you have to stop off at the babysitters to pick up the kids. And then on home for tea in a village not far from that place famous for its tea, Grantchester. Stands the church clock at ten to three and the table laid on the lawn.

But that was Rupert Brooke and his gentle England.

This was the England of a hoodlum who went out armed on a wet afternoon to rob and then for no particular reason, push a woman into a cupboard and shoot her. Not once but four times, he boasted to Maureen.

It was not a movie-style getaway car ready for any chase. In fact, it was so clapped out that they had to push start it.

As they hurried to the babysitters and then home for tea, Mrs Smith was still in the cupboard.

The Greek romantic and robber had fired at point blank range. Three bullets were fired into her head and neck and even at that range the fourth missed and went into the cupboard.

He had left her for dead, or so he thought. Yet she was not dead. She had guts and her courage took her from the cupboard along the floor of her shop and to the front door and out into the street.

It was a long, agonizing crawl by a woman who was

near death. But she was still conscious and could talk. She did not die for eighteen days.

By that time her murderers were away. They had gone back to her mother's where they discovered the amount of the riches they had killed for. Four hundred and fifteen pounds. Out of that had to come the petrol money, the cost of the bullets and the fee for the babysitter.

Next morning as Mrs Smith lay fighting for her life in Addenbrooke's hospital in Cambridge, they were off to the Continent, push starting their van to get going.

They went to Amsterdam where they read of Mrs Smith's death.

Maureen, her pregnancy now confirmed, wanted to come home and accept what she had done. Her lover would not hear of it. He rejected her claim that she could not live with what she had done. He would not let her go and he stopped her from returning to England by the simple means of taking her passport from her.

When they moved to Athens he made doubly sure by locking her in the house. But he could not keep her there forever. She was in touch with her mother and she sent her money and then, joy of joys, she found her passport.

She flew straightaway to Heathrow and gave herself up to the police.

It was in June in prison that she gave birth to her daughter.

And it was just after that that she volunteered to help catch her lover.

She pretended in phone calls to him that she was free and staying at her mother's. It was the police's idea after he began to ring Maureen's mother's home to talk to her. They realized that he did not know she was in custody and that they could use this to their advantage to trap him.

They took Maureen to Stapleford for the next time he rang. There were several calls before she finally agreed to meet him but in Amsterdam, not Athens.

The Dutch and Belgian police were alerted and dates

fixed. George was suspicious, not because he suspected that Maureen was under arrest but because of his nature. He was a roamer and a loner when he was not with a woman. He wanted to make sure there was no kind of trap.

He avoided airports and instead took a train to Paris. From there he rang the Amsterdam hotel where Maureen was supposed to be staying and it was the staff, primed to tell the right story, who said that Maureen was feeding the baby and would ring back. George was still worried so he switched plans and named Antwerp as the place where he would meet up with his mistress and new child for the grand reunion.

The police switched their tactics too and the Greek was arrested as he stepped down from the train.

From the start he protested his innocence. It was not him, he said. He had not, would not, do such a thing. When it happened he was not there at all. He produced a detailed timetable of his movements on the day of the murder, showing where he was and that at the time of the crime he was shopping in Cambridge.

But he had not counted on Maureen. She could not stomach what had happened and told all. She gave evidence against him in detail.

And when the jury went out there was added drama – the lights went out. Workmen accidentally cut off the electricity so the jury had to consider its verdict by candlelight. It took them over six hours to convict the Greek by a majority verdict of eleven to one.

They also found him guilty of robbery. Maureen was acquitted on the charge of murder because the prosecution did not offer any evidence against her. She admitted to the robbery.

Mr Justice Farquharson told her that he was impressed by the help she had given the police and that she had given evidence. He said that he had no doubt that 'your present degradation stems from your involvement with dangerous drugs' but she must be aware of the seriousness of the crime she had committed.

He jailed her for five years, a light sentence which took into account the fact that not only had she lured her ex-lover into the hands of the police but had given the evidence that had convicted him. George on the other hand said she was to blame. She was, her counsel said, utterly penitent and would not commit another crime. She was taken down and the judge turned to the Greek whose relatives were sitting in the public gallery.

The judge started by saying that he had not the slightest doubt about the jury's verdict and then sentenced the Greek to the mandatory life sentence and said that it was so appalling a crime that he should serve a minimum of twenty years which means that he would not be considered for release until he had spent that length of time behind bars.

It was a just punishment for a 'murderous assassination', as the judge described it.

George Farmakopoulos reacted instinctively. He screamed he was innocent and lunged at the police officers sitting near him. He tried to climb out of the dock and it took four prison officers to grab him and eventually get him out of the dock and down to the cells. As they did so his family in the gallery erupted and screamed abuse at the judge.

He ignored it as police stopped the noise and praised Detective Superintendent George Sutherland who led the hunt for the skill he and his team had shown. The detective had told the judge that there had been no deal with Maureen over dropping the murder charge.

There was no need. The enormity of what she had been involved in was too much for her. Some said that it had brought her to her senses. Perhaps it had. But it brought to an end her association with the Greek and took her off drugs and brought her down to earth with a very heavy bump.

Five years is a long time when you have little children, come from a good home and are used to a good style of living.

So what was the attraction, why did she fall for this Adriatic charmer?

Her counsel, Gilbert Grey QC, tried to explain it. She was, he said, rather a feeble character who had a twin relationship with the Greek: part fascination, part fear.

He said, 'He is a dangerous, unpredictable psychopath. The tragedy is that she had not fled from him earlier.

'He was, from time to time, fascinating and pleasant but looming over the relationship all the time was the prospect of violence which at any time could erupt.'

It was never so serious that it harmed Maureen. With Mrs Smith it was quite different.

The poor woman never had a chance. There was no reason for it.

It was typical of the kind of crime that occurs in this part of England. Post office robbery is ripe. Sometimes murder occurs when a postmaster has a go at the burglars and is shot for his pains.

Mrs Smith did not do this. She was shot for being there and but for the courage of his accomplice he might still be out of the country, drinking and chatting up girls and women in the bars of Athens with a notch on his gun.

4 Tickell

Mace-swinging Landlord

Kim Tickell was behaving like Basil Fawlty before Fawlty was invented. He was an outrageous publican, an outspoken landlord with an impeccable family background, had been to public school, been a judge's marshall, an army officer and an amateur actor. He tried one or two jobs and then settled down to run the Tickell Arms at Whittlesford just outside Cambridge. It was the family pub and he ran it to his taste (his second Christian name after Joseph was de la Taste which he pronounced with rich fruitiness when he answered the phone) to the delight of the undergraduates who flooded out there on bikes or in cars, and to the annoyance of some older people who went to the pub and found it not quite to their liking.

For Kim was different. He wore a monocle and eighteenth century knee breeches with silver buckled shoes. He had a camp style and voice, and his staff often consisted of sailors on leave. He had Royal Cavalier King Charles spaniels which ran with him as he strode round the pub and the village like the squire which many considered he was. He had a sharp tongue, softened usually with humour, as on the occasion when a young man, now a very senior executive in the newspaper world, asked him what his dogs were as they scampered past. Kim, immaculately turned out as ever, regarded the young man for a moment and then said: 'They are Royal Cavalier

King Charles spaniels and they possess one thing you do not – breeding,' and walked on.

The background music in the pub was often Ravel and he went through stages with the decor, favouring sawdust and gentile scruffiness as the pub became more and more of a cult place to go. It was a place to be seen in, a place at which part of the fun was to provoke Kim and be insulted in return. The banter at the bar was two way, but there were some customers he could not abide or banned. There were certain types he could tell at a glance and he would roar, 'I'm not having south London garage proprietors and their tarts in here. Get out!'

Others as they came through the door would be ordered straight out with 'Out, out, out, out!'

He did not like left-wingers, hippy types, scruffy types, blacks for a long time, anyone with a CND badge ('They stand for everything I detest') and Communists.

And anyone in bare feet.

It was this that landed him in the dock at the Assizes to face a charge of malicious wounding, the next one down after attempted murder, and also possessing an offensive weapon.

In keeping with his character the offensive weapon was a medieval mace.

It all happened on a lovely summer's evening in June 1970.

The pub was full and customers had overspilled out onto the lawn in front of it and from his bedroom window Kim surveyed the happy throng as they drank his special punch and other drinks. He went down and put on the Ravel and chatted with customers, and the air was full of smoke and bonhomie.

Then Kim noticed a party with a local company director and spotted that one of the girls, the director's daughter, was not wearing shoes. He asked her to put them on. Just how he said it is lost in the mists of time but it annoyed the director, Mr X, who came back to the bar thirty minutes later.

Mr X told the jury at Chelmsford Assizes when the case came up for trial in October 1970 that Tickell, 52 at the time, had said, 'If you have a comment to make about the way I run my establishment now is the time to get it off your chest.'

Mr X said he had a comment to make and picked up his beer glass to finish his drink.

'When I looked up I saw Tickell had raised the knife with the blade pointing at me. He started to bring the knife down toward me and I fended the knife off with my left hand and then tipped my beer over him. My hand was cut across my fingers and thumb. I turned to leave and he leaned across the bar and struck me again with the knife, cutting my upper left arm.'

He said he went outside bleeding badly from the nasty wound high on his left arm. Kim had used a carving knife to inflict it.

It was then that events became very out of the ordinary, for Kim grabbed a medieval mace off the wall of the pub and rushed outside swinging it like a soldier used to do in the middle ages on the battlefield.

'Is anyone next? I will take on anyone here,' he shouted, but receiving no takers he rushed back inside the pub, alleged Mr X.

Kim's version was different. He went into the witness box with a monocle on a chain around his neck and a carnation in his button hole. He was beautifully dressed in a grey suit. In his educated voice he denied wounding Mr X with intent to cause him grievous bodily harm and denied grabbing the mace with the cry 'gave me my mace and halberd'.

He said that that night had been one of the busiest of the year and during it he asked one of the girls in Mr X's party to put her shoes on. She did not and a few minutes later he asked her again and there was a short exchange with the party which resulted in Kim asking the party to leave because he did not like bad language in his pub. They went out but shortly afterwards Mrs X returned and began shouting at some of the staff.

She accused Kim of being a 'queer' and the pub being 'full of queers'. Mr X joined her and was glowering. Kim said that when he spoke to Mr X he still had the carving knife in his hand because he was cutting meat and had only broken off to smooth the trouble. Mr X suddenly picked up a glass on the bar and, 'He tipped it up and in a flash shot the contents into my face. After hearing a crash of broken glass I reacted automatically. I had the knife in my hand. Through the haze I saw a hand come down and up. I put my left arm in front of my face and the right hand holding the knife out to ward off any blow.'

'I only had one thought and that was to defend myself.'

He said he did not intentionally mean to strike at Mr X and was not even aware that he had cut him.

As Mr X left the pub, his wife came back in and hurled a spirit tumbler at him but it missed.

He went to have a look and outside he saw a scene he did not fancy at all. He explained, 'There was a group forming of rather long haired hippy types who I do not normally have in my pub. They were forming a very menacing group.'

So back into the pub he went to get his trusty mace and halberd.

He went on, 'I took the mace and halberd off the wall behind the bar and I went out … I remained in the doorway to stop them coming back. It was a show of force.'

He wanted to show it to the group who were behaving unpleasantly to a group of girls.

He said, 'I wanted these people who were making a scandalous scene to leave my pub. I thought they would come in and smash the place up from the way they were behaving.'

He denied that he swung the mace above his head and shouted. But he did say about his rule on shoes:

'I have a large notice up. I got rather tired of people flopping around with their large bare feet.'

Kim was defended by John Marriage, one of the leading barristers in the country then, who said the jury might think the scene when Mr X tipped beer over Tickell was like a scene from a Laurel and Hardy film but what happened afterwards was very serious because the charge was only one step below attempted murder.

The jury of ten men and two women were out for over two hours and came back to acquit him of wounding, but guilty of possessing an offensive weapon, the first man to be convicted of having a medieval mace in modern times in that way. He was fined £50, had a slight ticking off from the judge, and was warned not to do it again.

'Be assured I won't, my Lord,' he told Mr Justice Willis. Kim, related to a high court judge, was a relieved man and went back to the pub which had been with his family for over 250 years, to celebrate with champagne.

He recalled the words of his counsel as he made a final speech to the jury.

'This was an eccentric personality in an emotional state, striking the pose of a medieval squire, rushing to defend his home and castle, struggling to maintain his dignity and composure when he had lost both.'

Kim was just glad it was over. He said he was pleased he had been vindicated and the bare foot rule would stand just as it had always done. People in bare feet would be asked to put their shoes on.

But he had learnt his lesson about taking the law into his own hands.

He said: 'At the merest hint of trouble I shall call the police. I shall expect them to come out immediately. I have always found them to be very fair.'

Fair they were and there was no more trouble at the Tickell Arms which he continued to run in the family tradition, pushing their ownership up towards three hundred years.

He died in 1990 aged 73 after a long illness which he bore courageously and outrageously to the end. He was unmarried and left a million. The mace went back on the wall and stayed there.

5 'L'

Byron's Killing Pool

It was nearly five hours before Rupert Brooke's magical myth of Grantchester – stands the church clock at ten to three and is there honey still for tea?' – on a brilliant January day that the animal-loving fisherman met the gunman out for pheasants and brids in the idyllic woodland around Byron's Pool on the edge of the village. The pool was named after the poet who was an undergraduate at Trinity and the scene was a setting that morning that would have thrilled film makers and romantic novelists.

It was such a setting that provided yet another offbeat crime of violence that makes the area different.

That day the gunman (we shall refer to him as 'L') was in the cinema in Cambridge crying at 'Jaws', not because the film was upsetting him but because of what he had done.

The other man, a member of the League against Cruel Sports, was dead, and police were looking for the man who shot him three times. The first two shots were from a little distance, the last, after reloading, was at point blank range and blew half his head off.

Such were the facts of the morning. There was no romance, no soft words to fit the day. Just mindless bloody violence and murder for no apparent reason. At the worst, the occasion needed a punch, nothing more.

Instead, a sawnoff shotgun filled the air five times, two at birds, three into William S., aged fifty-one, father of two and a catering worker at the university.

That was at ten o'clock, a little time after Mr S. had arrived in his car, covered with anti-blood sport stickers, for a day's fishing and photography of birds on his day off. He set up his rods and then his camera and settled down in the sunshine, wrapped against the chill of the wind, for a good day out.

But at ten he heard two shots ring out and echo in the air. He set off to remonstrate with the person firing the gun, because he was obviously trying to kill some of Mr S.'s beloved birds.

A short time later a police constable, Neil Everard from Essex, arrived for the second day running. He had had such good fishing the day before that he wanted to repeat it before the weather broke.

He noticed a car that he had seen the day before parked in the same spot.

He was halfway to the pool from his car when he saw what he thought was a pile of rubbish with a wellington boot sticking out of it.

He went on to the side of the pool and found a bait box open, a rod on its rest and beside it a vacuum flask and in the mud a camera. There was no sign of the fisherman.

Being a good copper he was suspicious and had a look round. He saw that there was a trail from the path to the undergrowth where he had seen what he thought was a discarded wellington. It looked to him as though something heavy, something like a body, had been dragged along.

By the place where the leaves had been disturbed he found blood. Half hidden under them was the unfortunate Mr S.'s body.

Professor Austin Gresham, the Home Office pathologist, was called in to do the post mortem once the formalities of a murder inquiry had begun – the photographing of the scene, the examination of the body and the surrounds for clues, the removal of the body, the interviewing of witnesses which was helped considerably by the alertness of PC Everard and his exact memory of what he had seen.

The pathologist, veteran of many similar occasions, knew that Mr S. had a heart condition that could have killed him at any time but it was obvious that his heart condition had nothing to do with his death.

The first two shots that had hit him would not have caused death either, he told the police – and later the jury at Norwich crown court when the killer denied murder to the jury.

He and ballistics expert Geoffrey Brunt from the Nottingham forensic science laboratory, were agreed that the first shot from a Hungarian-made sawnoff shotgun was probably the one that hit him in the back, scattering the shot and suggesting that he was running away from the man with the gun.

At that moment it is unlikely that he feared for his life, but was afraid of being seriously injured.

The second shot when he was in full stride caught him in the left leg, through his rubber wading boot. The range was about seven yards.

The third shot, after the gun had been reloaded, was from a range of just a few inches to two yards maximum. It was fired while Mr S. was lying on the ground and completely blew away the left side of his head.

But who had done it? It did not take long for the police to arrive at the home of Peter 'L' off Histon Road in Cambridge. He was twenty-four and married. He was a cavity insulator and was known to the police. He was on a suspended sentence for possessing a firearm and ammunition after committing a crime.

He also had a car which matched the description that PC Everard had given of the car he had seen two days running at the pool.

'L', father of two, gave a version of what he had been doing that day and when he stood in the dock at Norwich, the jury of seven men and five women heard what they were from Mr William Howard QC, who was prosecuting.

They are interesting because they show how a person, accused of a horrible and apparently motiveless slaying changes his story. The first explanation was that he was at home.

Then came the second. Detective Chief Superintendent Charles Naan, then head of Cambridgeshire CID, conducted it and in it 'L' said that he had been at Byron's Pool between 9.15 and 10.15 on the morning of the murder, sitting in his car and eating his sandwiches. Then he heard some bangs which he thought came from the rifle range at Barton Road which was not far away. He explained that he lied in his first statement because he was frightened.

The detective, who had caught the Cambridge Rapist and had been involved in the Moors Murder when he was a young detective in Manchester, kept probing. First 'L' said he would like to telephone his wife. After that Chief Superintendent Naan said:

'I can see you are telling the truth. Why did it happen?'

'L,' said he was frightened. Then he offered to show them where the gun was, where he had thrown it into the River Ouse fifteen miles away at Stretham. He then went on:

'His watch came off while I was dragging him. He was coming at me. I fired at him.'

'Did you shoot him in the face?'

'I shot him on the side of the head I think.'

'How did you manage to shoot him twice in the back?'

But that was enough questions. 'L' said that he thought it was time he had his solicitor, Mr Howard told the jury.

Late that evening 'L' 's wife came to see him and asked him straight out, 'Did you do it?'

'Yes.'

'Why?' she asked and in his answer there was no explanation for the pointless killing of a fisherman out for a day's sport and photography.

'Who knows why,' 'L' said. 'That's one question I cannot answer.' Nor did he in statements to the police and the jury.

Then his wife asked him about the gun for she knew that he had an air gun but she did not know he had a sawnoff shotgun. He had had it for a long time, he said, and of course he had kept it hidden from her.

'It was an accident,' he explained to her, 'if only he had left me alone. I did not mean to kill him.'

All the time he was changing the story a little, coming a little nearer to what really happened. Perhaps he did not want to admit to himself what he had really done. Why does a man out shooting birds fire not once, not twice, but three times, reloading to finish him off? It was not like Taylor, the jealous lover in Newmarket, who finished his rival off because he could not bear to see him suffer like a mortally wounded animal, was it? (See Chapter 9.)

'L' made a third statement. This time his solicitor was there. The killer said:

'I had the gun in the boot of the car. I took it out and was just shooting at some small birds and tree stumps. I was sort of minding my own business.

'I was facing the river. Next thing I knew this fellow was ranting and raving and running at me. I didn't even know what he was saying. I was frightened.

'The gun went bang. I pulled him into the woods and things kept falling out of his pockets. I just could not believe I had done it, then I got panicky. I suppose you would if your gun had just gone off bang and you had killed a man and things fell out of his pocket as you dragged him off into the woods.

'His watch came off, his wallet and car keys dropped out of his pocket. I dropped my gun.'

After that he picked it up, went to his car with the dead

man's possessions and drove to Stretham where he threw everything into the river. It was recovered when he took police to the bridge to show where he dropped them. He went back to Cambridge where he threw his shoes into a rubbish bin, had a cup of tea in a cafe and then went to see *Jaws* at the cinema.

'I sat there crying for most of it. Now I am relieved it's all over. I didn't mean to kill him.'

So far he had admitted firing one shot. The next day he told his brother who came to see him at the police station that he had shot the man.

'I fired at him. The bloke came running and I fired. It was so quick.'

Mr Howard commented as he ended his opening address to the jury:

'It may be that he went to Byron's Pool to shoot pheasants or any other game that he might see and it may be that his presence there with a sawnoff shotgun aroused some indignation in Mr S., and perhaps Mr S. reproached or even shouted at him.'

Whatever they did resulted in 'L' putting his gun close to the fisherman's head and pulling the trigger to blast half his head off.

'You cannot put a shotgun within inches of a man's head and then pull the trigger without intending to kill,' the prosecution said, stating the obvious.

The jury were never to hear 'L' 's explanation of what really happened because he exercised his legal right not to give evidence. No accused person has to say a word on their own behalf in their own defence. It is not held against them and the judge, in his summing up, always makes a point of explaining this to a jury. But it is only human nature, and some might say commonsense, for members of a jury to wonder why the person in the dock does not give his side of what happened. He is only tried once and if he has denied the crime as 'L' had done it seems ridiculous not to say why you are not guilty of murder, to tell what really happened and emphasize that it was not murder. And – in a case like 'L' 's – explain how the gun went off, whether in a struggle or by accident, or perhaps the gun fell and went off by hitting something on the ground thus causing the fatal wound.

But 'L' did none of this. Clearly on legal advice he stayed in the dock and silent. Instead Mr John Marriage QC, a chairman of the bar council who tragically died at the age of 53, did all the talking for him.

He first admitted that 'L' was at the pool, that he fired a shotgun 'with the result that the deceased was struck by pellets and in fact died'.

The jury had heard that there had been five shots, first two, suggesting that those were the ones that alerted and annoyed Mr S., then three more with time for reloading between shots. They had heard that just firing an airgun had not been enough for 'L'. He wanted something more substantial like a shotgun. They had heard that he told his brother, 'I'm not making excuses because I shot the bloke.' That when police searched the area they found a shot pheasant and cartridge cases.

The jury wanted to hear what it was all about, why it happened.

Mr Marriage put forward a theory that the first two shots were because 'L' was not taking care as he shot birds.

Then, not knowing or caring that he had shot Mr S. accidentally, he wandered off in a world of his own and reloaded as he went, not realizing that Mr S. was in the wood, and when the irate fisherman ran up behind him he swung round and again accidentally, shot him in the face.

It was for the jury to consider whether it was an accident or deliberate. If they had any doubts they should acquit for there was a mystery about what happened. It was clear from his statements to the police that he had not meant to shoot the dead man, that it was an accident.

But the jury did not accept this. They found him guilty

of murder and he was sentenced – as he had to be – to life imprisonment.

He took with him the answer to the mystery, if indeed there was one, that the jury would have liked to hear. For they must have wondered why he fired three times. Once they could understand, a pull on the trigger in surprise when Mr S. shouted at him, a reaction, or in anger not thinking straight or caring about the result. But to fire two shots was one too many and to fire two and then reload, walk over to the wounded man and pull the trigger again from just a few inches and blow his head to pieces is taking the debate of shooting birds and cruel sports to a terrible conclusion.

6   Cook

The Cambridge Rapist

Jane was in a hurry that lunchtime, not a tearing hurry, but she did not have all that much time when she reached her bedsit in Pye Terrace on the eastern side of Cambridge by the River Cam. She was at the local technical college which was quite a bike ride away, but the journey was worthwhile to read the letter from her boyfriend that she was sure would be there and to write a quick reply before cycling back and posting the letter on the way.

She sat down at the table and began to read. But as she did so she was aware that someone else was in the downstairs bedsit. She turned and gave a half scream that was frozen in her throat by the sight in front of her.

There was a figure with a knife, a small stocky figure, not much more than five feet four inches tall, but what made him so much more terrifying was what he wore.

He had a black mask on with zips over slits. Worst of all was the fact that over his eye slits was written – in clear white capital letters – the one word:

RAPIST.

In his hand was a knife and he held it to her throat and told her that the name on the mask, so lovingly tailored, was his way of introducing himself. It saved having to explain just who he was although the girl knew who he was as soon as she saw him.

He had been terrorizing Cambridge since 18 October

1974 and this was the beginning of May.

He unzipped the slits to speak and look. The mask was made of an old leather shopping bag in the workshop near his caravan home some miles outside the city. It thrilled him to make it after seeing the wanted poster of himself which was on the door of the wine merchants where he worked as a delivery man. It added to his ego, to his power. He added hair round the bottom of the mask to give the appearance that he was both long haired and bearded.

He made the mouthpiece from a heavy industrial zip with long saw teeth so that when he pulled it open it gave the appearance of shark teeth, and then when closed again the most horrifying of Hallowe'en masks.

The girl was stunned by shock into submission as he whisked the knife around and told her to undress. He spoke softly, humiliating her. Then he raped her and was not content with that. He had been in the flat the day before, yet another break-in, and had had a good look round and knew what her name was and what personal possessions she had. One was her radio. He smashed it in front of her before leaving the deflowered virgin weeping and shocked as he vanished as quietly as he had arrived.

It was the seventh rape since he began almost casually in October because he had gone to rob and had stayed to rape. The girl was wearing just her dressing-gown and he took his opportunity.

From then on he continued his campaign and was extremely successful. The police worked flat out to catch him but he evaded him. There were several reasons (and we will come to another of them later) but one was his encyclopaedic knowledge of the streets, alleyways, short cuts and byways of Cambridge, particularly in the suburbs and bedsit land. When he was finally caught the police were astonished not only at his knowledge but that such routes existed. They appeared on no map.

On 6 May the ambulance passed the rapist as he made

his escape. He heard the siren above him on the Queen Elizabeth bridge over the Cam as he headed for freedom on the towpath.

Minutes later the police went to a boatyard and marina not far from the bedsit where Jane (not her real name) had been raped. They went to interview a man who they knew should be there, for he was one of their prime suspects, if not the prime suspect, as the rapist who had made international news. Cambridge is a name that is known all over the world in academic and other circles and brings visitors from everywhere. It is far more respected abroad then it is here. The fact that the university city had a rapist running riot, bringing fear of an unprecedented kind to bedsit land in particular with 15,000 girls there and the town in general, was big news.

The suspect was there. His name was Peter Samuel Cook. He was 47, and married but could not have children because he had no sperm count. He was also a lifelong thief. He was cocky with it and liked to leave messages on dressing-table mirrors. He could get in and out of almost any normal house and certainly any bedsit or small flat.

The police arrived in force but they met with failure because the two senior men in the firm gave him a watertight alibi. They said that he had been there all lunchtime looking at boats – for he had a luxury cabin cruiser called Margaret Rose after his wife. It had a 50 horsepower motor, was ocean going and equipped with all navigational aids for such trips. It was moored upriver at Upware, on the way to the sea in The Wash. Cook had never left the place. They had personally seen him there all the time.

They were absolutely sure and the police went away.

Their evidence however was quite useless. Cook had been there during his lunchtime but not throughout all his lunchtime. He had slipped away for just a few minutes; just long enough to don his disguise; pedal his ladies' cycle furiously alng the towpath to Pye Terrace (near the old radio and television factory), break into the bedsit, rape the girl and return to be back on the marina site when the police arrived. It suited his style to do such a thing. It was part of his act, his bravado, his satisfaction.

I said his first attack was on 18 October when he went to rob and stayed to rape but his crime wave of rape and robbery, humiliation and violence that increased attack by attack certainly didn't start then.

What led to it started many years before when he was nine. His first crime was burning down his father's shed and tying up schoolfriends and throwing things at them. Then he turned to theft and became such an unruly child that he was sent to an approved school as out of control. His parents – decent, hard working people – could not cope. He eventually broke their hearts.

His juvenile career as a thief became an adult one. But at the same time he had talent in building and design and when he was not a criminal he was a skilled, inventive and able workman who was in great demand.

He had absences because as a house and shop breaker he was not a great success. He was insolent with it but eventually he overplayed his hand and was caught.

In 1952 he was sentenced to five years at the old Quarter Sessions sitting in the Shire Hall at Cambridge. Cook was an extremely fit and athletic man and the prospect of five years was something that he did not fancy so he got his two colleagues who had also been sentenced to five years to form a ladder so that he could clamber up to the skylight in the cell in which they were being held. He managed to force it open and escape. The skylight was nine and a half feet from the ground.

Instead of vanishing and keeping out of the way he indulged in a game with the police, taunting them with letters to the local paper and tormenting the then head of the city CID, Detective Inspector Joe Breed. He told him that he had been in and out of Cambridge while on the run and then sent him a telegram to say the police should watch a certain house and they did, putting a number of officers in the area. A few days later Cook sent another telegram, suggesting that they looked inside another house close to the one he had named. They did and found he'd been inside to steal property.

The letter he wrote to the evening paper was in vivid blood red. His boast, however, was premature because he was arrested in Glasgow and brought back to Cambridge where he had two years added to his sentence to run concurrently for stealing women's clothing, including underwear, from a shop in Cambridge.

He served his sentence in Dartmoor when it was the most feared prison in England. It has a lower security rating now but then it was a terrible place, hated even by the most hardened criminals and by the prison officers and their families. Dartmoor in the winter is not the beautiful area that holidaymakers find in the summer.

Cook survived, his sense of humour, perverted as it was, helping him through it. He spent his years building, including a wall in which he put porridge bricks in one part so that if ever he wanted to escape he knew the weak spot of the wall.

His life after that long stretch inside was the same mix as before. He helped build a new shopping centre in the heart of Cambridge as the planners destroyed much of the beauty of the city when he was there. He travelled, being deported from Germany for stealing, from Switzerland for stealing, from several other European countries for dishonesty. In one he pretended to be mad and they said they quite understood but in their country they locked up madmen and threw away the key. Cook took the hint. Back in Britain he was convicted of breaking into university property and managed to talk himself into Broadmoor as mentally ill and in need of treatment. They discharged him after seventeen months as not being the sort of person who would respond to treatment. As Mr Justice Melford Stevenson said dryly at Cook's final trial:

'It is obvious that you have acquired a certain skill in talking to psychiatrists.'

Soon after he came out of Broadmoor he married a girl thirteen years younger than him. He was thirty-nine and she twenty-six, bigger than him and very much in love.

And outwardly Cook seemed to settle down. There was no more thieving, no more breaking and entering. He told his wife he could not have children because he had been injured in that department in a car crash in Germany and she accepted it. He used the car crash to explain the scars on his chest which were in fact the result of a breast operation. He worked on a development in the city and then as a delivery driver for a wine firm. His customers included a magistrate, who was later to be on the bench when he was sent for trial, and the police station where he would chat to the detectives and find out what the local crime gossip was. It came in very useful when they were looking for the rapist.

For six years he was clean, except that he was by nature a thief. He loved to use his skills to get into bedsits. He built up a comprehensive list of who lived where, how many were in a particular bedsit or flat, the phone number, the key number – for he knew where people kept duplicates in case they lost their original – and listing them all in his red hardback notebook. He scoured the adverts in the evening paper for bedsit vacancies and followed them up, detailing each one meticulously over the years.

He kept the books hidden along with other treasures in the shed near his caravan home which was opposite his parents' home at Hardwick, five miles outside the city. On view to all in the shed were the ships he modelled so exquisitely for his own delight. He spent hours in the shed, not all of it on modelling.

Cook was into hard-core pornography that he bought on the Continent as he ferried cabin cruisers back and forth for owners, a lucrative sideline. It was, it was said at his trial, the pornography that started him on the trail that ended with the Cambridge rapist attacking girls with a hideous mask on.

For three years he watched the films as he sold others to an eager trade in Cambridge. What he saw on the films attracted Cook tremendously. He was not very active with his wife but the filth he saw on the screen created a yearning in him to do the same. Some were sadistic, some just awful but one with a girl guide being raped was his favourite.

Finally, when he was in a bedsit, following his hobby of listing and matching ads for letting and girls who wanted rooms, he succumbed. Some believe it was a deliberate campaign, that he had been planning such a thing. Others – including the police – thought that when he told the girl that he came to rob but was staying to rape that that was the real answer. Cook found himself in a situation where he could live out the fantasy horrors he had seen in the seclusion of his shed and took the chance.

The girl was sitting on her bed in her dressing-gown in Springfield Road when the light went out. She asked if anyone was there and there was no reply. She felt the door being pushed and a voice said, 'Don't scream and no harm will come to you. I have a sharp knife.'

It was the start of something bad, something that became worse and created an atmosphere of fear that had never been known in the city before.

Just over a fortnight later, on 1 November, the rapist struck again. The girl was twenty and a student and she had just got out of her bath when the lights went out and she saw a figure in the doorway. It was Cook and he put an ether pad over her mouth and said, 'Shut up or I will kill you.'

He pushed her into the bedroom and then followed a sequence which became common to all his rapes, Mr John Marriage, QC, was to say when Cook finally appeared in the crown court at Norwich. There was humiliation in his tone, hands were tied behind the back, they were gagged, a knife came into play and nipples and breasts were bitten. In rape No. 2 he put his hands round her throat and said, 'So that was good.'

Unlike his first victim whom he tucked up in bed with her hands tied behind her back, he left this girl weeping and distraught.

The reign of terror had begun, Mr Marriage said a year later.

Thirteen days later a girl at Homerton College where she was a student went to practise the cello in the music room when the lights went out. Cook grabbed her and said, 'I'm going to murder you.'

He tied her, put a curtain over her head and led her to a shed and then partly undressed her so that he could bite her breasts and bugger her. He left her there after a string of humiliating, belittling words.

The police realized that they had something far above the normal run-of-the-mill attacker on the prowl. Each rape was getting worse, each rape was obviously committed by the same person and each time he struck, the violence increased.

The police put out a general warning to girls that they should be extra vigilant and that they should not go home alone at night.

There was a pause of a few weeks and then he struck again, on 8 December. The girl was woken with a torch being shone in her face. An ether pad was put over her mouth and he pricked her cheek with a knife. He marched her out into the garden and into a shed where he ripped her nightdress off with his knife and then raped her.

The violence was greater, the humiliation stronger. It was clear that they were as important to the rapist as the sex act. By this time the police knew what blood group he was and that he had no sperm count.

Every known criminal in the Cambridge area who was in the general height range of about five foot four inches, with a history of violence and sex attacks was seen and interviewed. Peter Cook had no history of violence.

On the night of 15 December, ten days before Christmas and as students were preparing for the Christmas holidays, the rapist had a field evening. He visited three houses and at one he suddenly appeared in the kitchen as an Australian girl was ironing. Her reaction was different to the others because she acted instinctively. She threw the iron and grabbed at the hair of the masked figure in front of her. To her astonishment it came away in her hand and the man vanished, his hair intact and in her grasp was a woman's wig.

That was to become important months later.

Cook went on to another house and finally to a bedsit in Huntingdon Road where he let himself in with a key and knifed the girl. He was wearing a wig and false beard and in his low, husky voice humiliated her, tying her, putting an eiderdown over her head and biting her breasts. She needed twenty stitches for her wounds and he left her in a state of extreme shock.

A week later Cook went to the police at their request and was cocky and jaunty. 'I wondered how long it would be before you wanted to see me. But I am 47.' And he held up the photofit picture in the local paper to compare it with him. They were looking for a younger man, a description built up from what the girls had told them. Remember that they had either not seen his face because of the darkness or because he was disguised. He was also a fit man for his age.

During the first few months of 1975 there was a lull in the rapist's activities. But that was for public consumption because there was real terror in bedsit land and it spread to all parts of the city. Dozens of policemen were out patrolling every night looking for him. Girls were told never to go home alone and boyfriends were always to be with them. Girls were told to lock up their bedsits to make sure that no one could get in. They were advised to buy chains because it was obvious that the rapist was often using a key to make his entry.

The two senior detectives in charge of the inquiry, Detective Chief Superintendent Charles Naan and his deputy, Detective Superintendent Bernard Hotson, knew that Cook was still around but at that stage, of course, they had no idea it was him. They knew the rapist was getting into bedsits and leaving messages on the mirrors like 'The rapist has called. Watch out' scrawled in vivid lipstick, just like the young housebreaker used to do back in the early fifties. It was one thing suspecting that it was Peter Samuel Cook, it was quite another to prove it. He was as slippery as any eel, as smart as any policeman (his bedside table had a copy of Moriarty's police law on it) and quick and knowledgeable when it came to outsmarting the law.

His actions created a state of lingering fear, one that never went away from the girls as they walked the streets back to their bedsits late at night, whoever they were with. We lived in a village just outside Cambridge and the daughter of one of our friends shared a bedsit with two other girls in the Huntingdon Road area of Cambridge where there are dozens of them. She and one of her friends arrived back one morning around three o'clock. The room was full of smoke and in an old ashtray on the table were the butts of roll-ups. There was a message too. The rapist had been there, waited and finally become fed up and left. The girl was petrified as were her friends. They went home and stayed at their homes with their parents until the rapist was caught. Thousands were in the same state and Cook revelled in it.

He did not actually rape again until April by which time his sense of the dramatic was matching his violence in intensity. He was all in black, a hood over his head and a zip for his mouth.

'Do you know who I am?' he asked his victim. 'I am the Cambridge rapist.'

He proved it and after the rape he trussed her up and it took hours for her to free herself and attract attention.

The police tried a new move. They asked all men five

foot seven inches and under to go to the police station to give a sample of saliva. There was one other qualification: they had to be under thirty because that was the age range they believed the rapist to be in. Cook was seventeen years older.

Dozens of young men came and gave saliva. The police were looking for a man who had no sperm, was an O group secretor with a PGM-2 factor which was exactly what Cook was and his medical records dated 1960 showed that. The police had no idea of this and why should they? He was outside the age range and no one came forward to tell them about his medical history.

Cook went on visiting bedsits, cycling into Cambridge in disguise and vanishing out again through the rings of police.

During the day he worked for the wine merchants but he also spent much time on his ocean-going cabin cruiser. He bought it when his father sold off land for £78,000, a vast sum, to building developers and gave his errant son whom he loved dearly a sixth of it.

In May Cook struck in Pye Terrace when he was ostensibly at the boatyard. It was the first time that he had used the hood with rapist painted on it. The violence had increased, the talk was more humiliating. He escaped.

The police were now certain it was Cook but they could not prove it. They found nothing when they searched his caravan home. Why should they? Part of his thrill was in matching them, then defeating them.

On 8 June, a month after Pye Terrace, a girl of twenty-seven who lived in a students' hostel, heard a tapping on her door in a corridor of rooms in the early hours of the morning. She called out to see who it was and then the door began to open.

It always brings a gasp in a crowded cinema. Imagine what it was like in real life when you knew that for eight months a rapist had been on the prowl.

She got out of bed and went to the door. She sensibly

had a chain attachment. She opened the door with the chain on and there saw the rapist with his mask on. He tried to force his way in, slashing with his knife as he did so, but the chain held and although she was cut she opened her mouth and screamed and screamed. It had two effects: the rapist took to his heels having chanced his arm in the most outrageous fashion, and people came running from everywhere, girls from other rooms, police, and two fishermen from the banks of the Cam.

The city was already ringed with policemen. There were policemen everywhere and the word was given to each of them on their pocket radios that the rapist had struck and was on the move.

Police were waiting at Hardwick surrounding the caravan and area.

But of Cook there was no sign. The little man who casually scrawled 'Sleep tight – the Rapist' after he had let himself in and found that no one was at home, had disappeared into the night.

On the outskirts of Cambridge, in a road where there are bedsits and university houses, Detective Constable Terry Edwards was on duty, waiting and hunting the rapist like so many of his colleagues.

Suddenly under the street lights he saw a woman pedalling fast towards him. She was wearing what appeared to be a fur coat and she had shopping-style bags on the handlebars.

His immediate reaction was that it was a student hurrying home, going as fast as possible because of her fear that the rapist might be about.

He called on her to stop but she did not slow. He stood in the road in front of her but she kept coming. He shouted again and as she did not stop as she came level with him, he made a grab to stop her.

A wig came away in his hand. The woman was the rapist in full disguise.

Edwards leapt and brought the woman down from the

bike, calling for help on his pocket radio. The woman struggled but he held her.

When help arrived in just a few seconds, the woman stood up. Layer after layer came off to reveal Peter Samuel Cook. In his shopping bags were the rapist's gear: hood, knife, women's clothing, ether pad.

It was, as Cook would have said as an expert criminal, a fair cop.

To his credit he admitted everything. He told DCS Naan and DS Hotson, 'I must be mad because I am talking myself into life imprisonment.'

He took the two senior detectives on a tour to show them the places where he had been to rape and visit, the back alleys, the ways in and out of Cambridge and most important of all his hiding place in the shed at Hardwick.

In exchange for this the detectives who were in a state of euphoria and relief – 'we've got him, we've got him' was the jubilant cry over my telephone at four in the morning that Sunday as I was told that it was all over and girls could sleep soundly again – allowed him to go back to the caravan for the last time and see his pets. Cook was a realist. He knew he was going to be an old, old man if he ever came out again.

It was the shed that fascinated the police. The treasures of infamy were later laid out down at the police station and it was a dreadful collection.

There were six hundred or so different items hidden under the floorboards.

The prize of the collection was his red notebook which listed the names of dozens of flats, the girls in them, the phone numbers, plans of the layouts and the key numbers. In dozens of air-tight tins and plastic bags were the keys by the hundred. There were keys to fit the locks, there were skeleton keys to fit other locks, there were keys to colleges and hostels for he collected keys like a magpie, each labelled immaculately. His collection showed that he had visited every street in bedsit land in a city of bedsits.

Also in his private Black Museum were porno films, the dark glasses and blonde wig he wore when riding to his last successful rape, sexual aids, a large collection of women's clothing, 22 different wigs, shoes, boots, underwear and cosmetics, jewellery and other accessories – and a passport with £100 in pesetas in it, ready for an escape to Spain, his favourite country, in his cabin cruiser.

And with this were the items that he carried for his last raid: the mask with its frightful slits, an assortment of wigs, a torch with spare batteries, tissues, two watches, his cigarette making kit, a sheath knife with its sheath, a razor sharp bread knife, an ether pad and ether, two jemmies, a selection of women's tights, another selection knotted into a rope, a bunch of skeleton keys, a special tool for fusing lights, a hairbrush, a collection of women's underwear, dresses, shoes, wigs, make-up and a pair of training shoes whose imprint had been found at the scene of some of the rapes.

It was the evidence that the police needed, the evidence that made Cook confess, the evidence that was essential because without it there was nothing to prove that Cook did them. There might be circumstantial medical evidence but they had to be certain. Crooked and wicked he may have been but he was as sharp and as twisting as any criminal with years of experience of evading the law could be.

As the people of Cambridge woke up, and as girls woke and checked their security locks were still in place, the police were taking Cook on his final trip without the heavy guard of prison officers.

He told DCS Naan, 'You know it all. The only way out is suicide. What I have done to these girls makes me sick.'

There was no suicide but whatever his behaviour had done to him it was nothing to what it did to his father and mother and wife. They were more than sick. His mother died soon after, possibly from the shame and broken heart inflicted by her only son who had gone way past the thieving young man she once knew. His father was baffled. 'If I had known he was doing this I would have shot him,' he said.

Cook's wife could not understand it. On the last occasion that Cook appeared before Cambridge magistrates for committal for trial I met her at the police station where she went to see the husband she loved. Two of us spoke to her for twenty minutes or so and she talked quite happily about Cook. Their marriage had been fine, she said. He was not that keen on sex and she was willing any time he wanted to, and there was never any question of pornography or anything else like that. He was a good husband and she had absolutely no idea that he had been doing these terrible things. She could barely believe it and she was going to stick by him and wait for him to come out.

It was going to be a long wait, one for ever if the judge at his trial, Mr Justice Melford Stevenson, had his way. He told him, 'You showed no compassion for your victims, you used them to gratify your lust and you terrorized a very considerable community. I would not be doing my duty if I did not impose upon you for each count of rape life imprisonment and it is my opinion that in the context of this case life will mean life. Take him away.'

He is still inside (1993) and in his sixties. There is no reason why he should ever be released. A man sentenced to life thirty three years ago died recently, still serving his sentence.

Going back slightly in time, that summer Cambridge was a different place. Girls roamed happily and laughed and the tension lifted like a great curtain coming up to reveal sunshine and happiness.

Cook waited in prison on remand but there were stories that other prisoners had poured scalding water into his groin and that he had been hit. They may well have been true.

On 3 October he appeared at Norwich crown court and

it was all over in less than an hour and a half. Cook did as he said he would and pleaded guilty which spared his victims the final humiliation of giving evidence and then being challenged on it. Most, if not all, would have found it impossible to identify him.

He admitted six charges of rape, one of buggery and two of unlawful wounding. He looked a very average little man, a bit shifty but nothing out of the ordinary, as he sat in the dock. John Marriage, QC, went through the rapes one by one, his arrest and what he had said to the police.

The medical report from Leicester prison said curtly, 'There is nothing wrong in his head. He can be dealt with within the confines of the prison system.'

When he was released from Broadmoor, another report said, he was not a suitable person for that institution, meaning that he was sane and was not suffering from any mental illness.

Then Mr Brian Higgs told the judge the reason behind it all, giving Cook's explanation for the terrible things he had done.

It was all due to pornographic films. He bought a magazine two years before and that led to his interest in films. They depicted violence and obscene acts 'that he could not and would not practise' on his wife, he said.

But his addiction grew and he was driven to commit the first of the rapes.

Cook told his barrister, 'It was a living hell. The films control me.'

He had an uncontrollable urge to do what he had seen on the screen and did so. He carried the knives to frighten, not to hurt or injure, but it was the films that had triggered him off.

He knew that the girls must have been terrified by the acts he committed. He also knew what he was doing and had answered a television appeal by a psychiatrist to go and discuss his problem. Cook rang him and said that he was suffering from an inner conflict where half of him was trying to do right as the other half forced him to do wrong. They talked briefly and fixed an appointment but the rapist never turned up.

Mr Higgs, who had little he could say in mitigation, made the point that Cook had pleaded guilty thereby saving the girls from giving evidence, a matter for which he should be given credit.

And he mentioned that Cook's wife was standing by him, one of the remarkable aspects of the case. He told of a conversation between the two when Cook had been arrested (and what a shock it must have been for her to be woken in the early hours of Sunday morning to be told that her husband had been arrested as the Cambridge rapist, the most notorious criminal in Britain and Europe at the time) and she had referred to his blue films.

She said, 'I told you not to have them. I don't know why you did it.'

It was a question she was left to ponder as her husband was ushered down the stairs to the cell under the old building to await transfer to prison forever.

In Cambridge there was much hindsight detection. There always is but in this case the point was made that the police should have suspected the pint-sized Cook with his small penis and testicles and his criminal background as the obvious suspect and should have watched him like a hawk. There were letters in the local paper and some were very critical. One was from a man with a strong axe to grind because his son had been jailed for an attack on police at the football ground. Rumours abounded too that the detectives leading the hunt had dismissed Cook's name and said it was not possible that he could be responsible. There was no truth in that.

The trouble with hindsight armchair detection is that it is all too easy when you know the answers. You can say mistakes were made and if they had not been, the criminal would have been apprehended earlier.

But in the case of Cook it was difficult because the rapist

had to be caught. It is true that if they had known early on that the rapist was not in his twenties as the victims believed, and was a man of 47, they would have looked at Cook from the start. They did look at him as a potential suspect before Christmas but there was nothing to connect him with the rapes. He was a reformed thief and housebreaker who had no history of sex crimes nor violence. He was not known to be interested in sex and even if it had been known that he was an avid porno film viewer (or even smuggler from the Continent) it is doubtful whether it would have brought him any more into the frame. There were dozens of men around in that era when porn films were the 'in' thing and available anywhere.

At the same time police had a look at Cook's home and talked to his wife. Later a man walked into the police station – when they were becoming more and more suspicious about Cook without being able to prove anything – and admitted he was the rapist. He was one of many but he had gear in his car and he fitted the general description and he was confessing. It was not him. He was just one of the nutcases who enjoy admitting crimes they have not committed and waste police time.

In the spring the police were told by one of the victims, very near the time when Cook was caught, that the rapist could be in his forties. Cook was very high on the list of suspects. When the girl was attacked in Pye Terrace near the marina at lunch-time the first person the police went for was Cook but he was alibied out, not by one person, but two.

By that time there were dozens of policemen out every night waiting for the rapist. Cook was even more cunning in his visits and attacks. Police were watching the roads back to Hardwick and thought they had them all covered. They did not know them all like the rapist.

Men were waiting at Hardwick the night he was caught, riding a ladies' cycle dressed as a woman.

As one senior detective said after it was over, 'You cannot arrest a person without proof and we did not have any.'

They knew, as did Cook, who stripped and washed himself clean after every rape, that they had to catch him in the act, red handed or in his case, gear handed.

It was inevitable that in the end he would be caught because each trip boosted his ego and gave him a tremendous kick, a wonderful high, that he wanted more, always more. Now he can never have any.

7 Pratt

The Murder of One of the Richest Women in Britain

Rachel Parsons was a woman born outside her time. She was a brilliant engineer in the days when women were not and the glittering prizes that she tried for in politics and racing did not come her way. She died in not dissimilar circumstances to Miss Haversham in *Great Expectations*, in Newmarket at the hands of an ex-employee for the sake of a few pounds that she owed but would not pay from her vast fortune.

She was born in 1885, daughter of Sir Charles Parsons who invented the marine steam turbine and became fabulously wealthy through his skill. When he died in 1931 he left her nearly £1 million, an enormous sum then. Her grandfather was the Earl of Rosse, an astronomer and president of the Royal Society who discovered the spiral nebulae, luminous patches made by distant stars. She wanted to follow in her father's footsteps and went to Cambridge where she became the first woman to take the mechanical sciences tripos – and with honours – and then went into the family business. When her brother, whom she adored, went to the war she took his place in helping to run it and was heartbroken when he was killed in the trenches like so many others of his generation. She went on with the business until the end of the war, when she had to give up because in those days a woman's place was in the home.

She also had to give up, on the instructions of her parents, the man she loved, for they thought him not up to the standard they required for the husband of their daughter. How strange it is that parents then held such sway over their children. Now she would have told them to mind their own business and gone her own way. But she did as she was told and people who knew her well said that she never really got over it. She was always suspicious afterwards of men's motives, particularly when she became one of the richest women in Britain. Sadly her parents were very poor judges of her suitor's capabilities. He became a diplomat and internationally famous while she went downhill in an unhappy way.

In the early twenties she went into politics and became a member of London County Council, getting into the swinging social set, and holding exciting parties at her home in Grosvenor Square where everyone who was anyone went. She lived there for many years and then bought for £15,000 the lease of a magnificent house in Belgrave Square. It had many reception rooms as well as a ballroom. She lived there on her own although after she had been burgled she tended to stay in hotels. She sold the house to an international company in 1946 and bought No. 3, once the home of the Duke of Kent.

In that year she also bought Branches Park, a thirty-seven bedroom eighteenth century mansion in rolling grounds and wooded parkland. It had ten reception rooms, a swimming pool and extensive stables at Cowlinge, about eight miles from Newmarket, to go into racing.

She used the money she obtained by selling other property and in the next few years she sold her 10,000 acre estate in Ray, Northumberland, to the Ministry of Agriculture. For a mere £50,000 they had the land on which there were nine tenant farmers.

On top of that she bought Lansdowne House and its stables on the racecourse side of Newmarket and planned to take fourteen of her yearlings from Branches to be trained there for the 1955 season.

Her racing had been going well. She was one of the wealthiest owners and her best horse was Le Dieu d'Or which had a successful season as a two-year-old.

But as the years slipped by Miss Parsons changed. She had a beautiful voice which always surprised people who saw this tattily dressed woman with ill matching clothes, shabby furs, flat heeled canvas shoes and auburn wig under a huge Edwardian hat.

Her clothes matched the way she lived whch eventually became a life of squalor.

She did not like people much and she treated employees and shopkeepers with contempt, keeping them waiting for their money and abusing them. But she did love animals and one of her failings with her racehorses was that she overfed them. Even Le Dieu d'Or was overfed. She would slip out in the night and give him titbits.

Her favourite animal was an Airedale called Bruce who, once she had moved out, lived on his own in Branches, sharing the place with dozens of rats. She left the house and its 2,600 acre estate when she moved into Newmarket, rowing with the Jockey Club over the stabling of her horses and letting them wander in the yard, when the Jockey Club would not let them train on the heath.

Before she left Branches for the smaller Lansdowne House, Miss Parsons lived in only two rooms and in dirt. Potatoes and vegetables were dumped in the state banqueting hall, the linseed oil was in the linen cupboard and the two rooms in which she lived were full of rotting food and empty sardine tins and bottles.

When she left she returned daily to feed Bruce who kept guard among the broken egg shells and the expensive fur coats she left lying in the mess.

Her regular taxi driver said: 'She was a strange woman. Everyday I called for her and drove her to the stud farm at

Branches. She told me she was afraid to live in the house after burglars broke in in March [this was 1956] and finally moved into the Newmarket house.

'One day I went into the large room in which she was living, the only room in which she was living and it was littered with egg shells, Ascot hats and papers. She used to wear one nylon and one woollen sock with a hole in it.

'She was mad on films and used to go to the pictures in Cambridge three times a week. She used to carry about £300 in notes stuffed in her handbag and she would pay the men working for her with these notes. Often she would not pay until they asked.'

In those days £10 a week was a good wage for a workman.

'Her training establishment was overrun with rats and mice. She kept corn in one part of the house and it was altogether in a shocking state.'

Later Branches was demolished; such a ramshackle and terrible state it was in.

A neighbour of hers in Newmarket said, 'She wore a strange assortment of clothes. Her shoes were always dirty and down at heel and her stockings always appeared to be falling down. She did not give any outward impression of wealth.'

Nor did she give any inward impression either. She quarrelled with tradesmen, and argued with the council in court when statutory notices were served that she must repair her property.

At Branches she feared burglars and thefts by her staff and locked most of the rooms.

In consequence, the corn was kept in the servants' hall and the linseed in the linen cupboard so that the mice wrecked the expensive sheets, linen and eiderdowns, using the exquisite materials for nests.

Her eccentricity was as well known as her meanness. She kept a Jersey cow just to provide milk for her dog Bruce, and she used a taxi twice a week to fetch dog biscuits for him and her twenty-two cats.

And the first president of the Women's Engineering Society and the only woman to hold a master mariner's ticket would take her bath with just a hat on and call for a maid to turn the taps off when the water overflowed.

As the years went by and she lived off sardines and only turned out properly to see her horses race in her racing colours, light blue and violet stripes, she became a menace in dealing with staff, few of whom stayed.

She insisted loudly and sometimes with the lash of her horsewhip that she was the boss and she argued continuously with her employees over money, not paying until the last moment or even not at all. She was certain that she was surrounded by thieves and would rather drive into Newmarket to buy a small quantity of her beloved sardines or eggs than have any large amount in the house.

She quarrelled with all tradesmen, calling them thieves and robbers. They had difficulty in arguing with this brilliant, foul tongued woman who was a genius with figures. She kept them all in her head and would work out the wages and pay them out reluctantly and would always want the change, even if it was only a halfpenny.

So on 2 July 1956, the woman who seventeen years before had held one of the last great parties before the Second World War, at which royalty and very important people were guests, had reached almost the bottom. She was still very sharp at seventy-one, still wore her flower and fruit decorated Edwardian hats, still ranted and raved at staff, and still kept her pets and her horses, but she was run down and soiled like the beautiful estate at Branches which was going to dying seed and destruction.

She answered the knock on the door reluctantly and found on the doorstep one of her former stablemen, Dennis Pratt, aged twenty-six, who had been employed to help look after her string of ten horses. He was married with two children and his wife was expecting a third. He had worked for Rachel Parsons until May but when he left, she refused to pay him the two weeks holiday money he insisted he was rightly owed.

He had been to see her twice before and the police had been called and they told him to keep away. But he went back a third time, needing the money.

No one knew she was dead until the next day and then only because Pratt went into a jewellery shop in Cambridge, fourteen miles away, and offered to sell a pair of binoculars which he said belonged to his dead father. The jeweller asked him to call back after he had valued them and rang the police who were waiting when he returned for the money.

He said his name was Alan Poulson and he answered the questions the police asked. They had a look in his briefcase and two cameras and two travelling clocks were inside.

He was asked to go to the police station which he did. In those days, the Cambridge City police station was much nearer the centre, opposite the old New Theatre where many of the top music hall stars performed and which eventually closed after undergraduates let mice run on the stage during a nude show. Nudes were only allowed to be seen as long as they did not move. The mice sent them scattering from their podiums.

In the interview room Pratt turned out his pockets and on the table in front of him lay eighteen ten shilling notes and fourteen one pound notes, a total of £23 which was a considerable sum of money.

He was asked where he had got it.

He said, 'They are from Lansdowne House, Parson's, Rachel's,' and then he started to sob. He wrote down his real name and address and said, 'This will be a shock to you. I have done her in.' He went on, 'I went back to her house last night to get my holiday money.' This of course was just what the detective had warned him not to do and if he had just listened to that advice the old woman would have been alive and he would have been at home for the birth of his third child instead of facing the condemned cell. 'I asked her for it and she hit me with her handbag. She hit me a couple of times. I shouted at her to stop. I lost my temper and picked up a big iron bar from the ground beside the yard door. She carried on going for me with her handbag and I hit her on the head with the iron bar.'

Imagine the astonishment of the two detectives interviewing him. They thought they had a housebreaker at worst and instead they had a killer telling them how he had done it. More, they had a murder which had not been discovered.

They had a quick look at his clothing and there was a blood stain on his trousers. Pratt said, 'I think that is blood from the head when I tried to lift it.'

It was then they stopped him and rang Newmarket police and told them to go round to Lansdowne House and see if what Pratt was saying was true.

They could not find the body so Pratt was asked again and this time he gave exact directions to the place where he had dragged her – the pantry. It may sound silly that the police could not find the body but in recent years Hampshire police missed a body in a large garden during the night. If a murderer wants to hide a body it is not difficult. It it is hidden well enough it is often only through bad luck that it is found.

This time, the second time, Newmarket police found the body of the rich old lady.

Pratt then made a statement, In it he said, 'I picked her up by the shoulders and she was breathing heavily. She was real heavy. I did not know what to do. I stayed with her and felt her head. I did not know whether to run away or not.

'It was just getting dark at this time. I couldn't help her. I must have realized it was too late to help her. After I had stayed with her a little while and I had tried to sit her up she gave a heavy gasp like a gurgle or giggle and then she stopped breathing.

'I thought she was dead. I waited a little while and got her into the house by dragging her on her back into the back door.

'I didn't know what to do. I went upstairs and with the keys I had taken from her handbag I undid the bedroom door. The curtain was not drawn so I drew that and put the light on. I then listened for a while and heard a noise outside.

'I stayed for a while and then went downstairs again and stood at the back door. I was trying to make up my mind what to do. I remembered her handbag which was still in the passage so I went down to it and took it to the bottom saddle room where I closed the door, put the light on and had a look in the bag.

'I took the money from there and put it in my pocket. I then went back to the house, went up to the bedroom again and had a look around the room where I took two cameras, binoculars, two small clocks which you have here and some beads, pearly ones and pink ones and some others which are in a cocoa tin in my shed. I put them in a small case and I went out and locked the bedroom up.

'I then went downstairs and dragged her into the pantry. I knew she was dead. I reckoned she had died outside.'

When he locked the house and left, it was getting light and he thought it was about three in the morning as he cycled home. He put the case in the shed.

'I went in my house and had a cup of tea. After some time I went up to bed where my wife was asleep. When I woke up it was about five or six in the morning so I got up and went downstairs and made myself a cup of tea.'

And what next? He cycled back to Lansdowne House.

'I went in by the back door and went back to where I had put her, the pantry. She was lying in the same position and I felt her throat and she was dead cold.

'I closed the pantry door and went through the house again and went upstairs and turned the lights off which I had left on all night in the bedroom. I had left them on because she always slept with the light on and I opened the curtains which I had closed the night before. I locked the bedroom and came down the stairs again. I again locked all the doors and left the house.'

Before leaving he threw the iron bar into the coke shed and on the way home he bought some chocolate for the children. Later that day he tried to sell the binoculars and the police were called.

Pratt looked at the two detectives as he finished making his statement and said, in a phrase so many killers use, 'I can't realize that this has all happened. It was all like a dream.'

Dream to him but reality to everyone concerned. The murder was big news. She was a name, an extremely wealthy name and she had property and horses to be looked after, estates to be considered and executors to discharge her will.

As Pratt appeared before Newmarket magistrates and was remanded in custody, plans quickly were made to sell all her seventy horses. Her relations contacted each other to discuss the will and Bruce who had lived a lonely life in the sixty-eight room Georgian mansion Branches was let out and handed to estate workers.

There were obituaries too which told of her genius and achievements in an age when women were not supposed to have them, how her ambitions failed because of this, how her loneliness affected her, how kind she was but how she could not stand sycophants and fortune hunters, how easy it was to criticize her behaviour from the fireside chair without really knowing what it was like to be very rich and lonely.

Pratt kept appearing in court, being remanded back to Bedford prison until he was committed for trial at Newmarket magistrates court on 24 July. At that hearing his statement was read out and a taxi driver told how, just a few days before the murder, he drove Rachel Parsons to

Cambridge and back and when they arrived at her home Pratt was waiting.

The taxi driver said in evidence that Pratt ignored her threat that she would ring the police. He told her that he had come for his two weeks' holiday money she owed him but she told him to get out and he told her he would report her to the Labour Exchange, the old name for a Job Centre.

He was committed for trial for murdering the old woman by fracturing her skull and his counsel, John Marriage, said he was reserving his defence.

In August the details of her estate were published. She did not leave a will and her fortune of £612,000 – about £180,000 after duty – was shared by thirty relatives.

Three months later Pratt denied murder when he appeared in the dock at Chelmsford Assizes. The prosecution told the same story as they had at the magistrates court and Pratt's statement was read out again.

It was when Detective Sergeant Ronald Bigmore gave his evidence that the defence to the capital charge became clear. Michael Havers, defending the stableman at the trial, said that he would ask the jury to return a verdict of manslaughter on the grounds of provocation.

He asked the detective about the house and Rachel's way of life. He said that her house was neglected and unkempt, and inside thoroughly dirty. In the bedroom were hundreds of old egg shells littered everywhere and the bath was clogged with tea leaves. There were also hundreds of keys lying about, the ones she carried with her.

The detectives said that once she said two thousand pheasants had been stolen and when he said that she meant poachers, she said she meant thieves and set her dog on him which chased him off the premises.

Another witness for the prosecution, one of her former stablemen, said she was a bad-tempered woman and her former trainer, Charles Bell, said he lost three stones in weight working for her. He said she called him every name in the dictionary and was impossible to please as an employer. He added, 'I was the whipping boy.'

So when Pratt went into the witness box the jury had a very clear picture of the woman he admitted killing but not deliberately. They already knew of the kind of provocation he and anyone else who worked or dealt with her had to put up with. A well written obituary by someone who rarely saw the woman might read well in the lounges of those who buy the heavy prints but those who were on the ground and around her knew what she was really (and sadly) like in her closing years.

Pratt definitely did.

By this time his third child had been born. He had been in prison for several months on remand, knowing that he faced the rope if he was found guilty.

He told the jury how he looked after her favourite horses, Le Dieu D'Or, a difficult animal with a difficult owner. After he had left her employment he went back for the holiday money which he was owed.

'She told me to get out and that I was not going to get any money. She called my wife and I guttersnipes and said I had spoiled Le Dieu D'Or. She came for me and hit me on the head with her handbag. She was in a horrible mood.'

The stableman, a handsome looking young man, said he stood his ground.

'I told her not to be so silly and pushed her away. She was fuming and called me a tramp. She hit me a second time and I told her to stop.'

It was then he picked up the iron bar lying on the ground and hit her. 'I do not remember how many times I struck her, I can hardly realize I have done it now.'

He said that at the time he was composed, 'then all of a sudden she came at me ... I couldn't help it.'

He took the money and property to help his wife with the housekeeping.

When the judge, Mr Justice Diplock, asked him how he would describe Miss Parsons he replied without hesitation, 'stupid'.

The jury were told by the judge about the old woman. He said that they had been given a picture of an eccentric, quarrelsome, unpleasant old woman, dirty in her habits and uncontrolled in her language.

He went on: 'You may think that a reasonable man used to the eccentricities of this old woman would have made allowances and taken less seriously her words and actions than the words and actions of someone who was not an eccentric.'

The judge of course had never felt the sharp end of her violent and foul worded tongue nor had to go time after time to get the pittance, a handful of pound notes, he was owed while he was out of work and had a family to feed; he had not had to listen to her screaming abuse over her horse as she accused the staff of not feeding it and then getting up in the middle of the night to slip it titbits.

Judges are often criticized for not knowing about the real world. Here was an example. The judge added to his criticism of the defendant by saying that the jury might think his actions in dragging the old woman and leaving her body in the pantry as those of a 'guilty, cool customer'.

The jury took all this into account and decided that he had not premeditated her death but that he was guilty of causing it, bringing in a manslaughter verdict.

Mr Havers said that Pratt, a former apprentice jockey with no previous convictions, was below average intelligence. He read part of a report from a doctor to the judge in which the doctor said that Pratt had acted under the influence of powerful emotions which blinded him to what he was doing. It was unfortunate that there was a lethal weapon around when these emotions were aroused. What he was saying in layman's terms was that if there had not been an iron bar there he might not have killed her. But then he might not have killed her when he was warned off by the police on the two earlier occasions but still came back.

The judge used few words. He told Pratt, who had tears streaking down his face;

'The jury have taken a merciful view but that cannot disguise the fact that this was a very brutal crime.'

As he sentenced him to ten years Pratt broke down and sobbed and had to be supported by the two prison officers as they took him down to the cells.

.It was not quite the end of the story. A few days after Pratt's trial it was announced that Branches was going to be sold by the administrators of her estate.

When the sale was held on 12 December the estate failed to reach its reserve price. It was then sold privately and the next year it was announced that the new owners were to demolish the mansion, built in 1739.

Water from the roof was pouring through the ceilings and the structural damage and the interior mess made it unusable for anything without a vast amount of money being spent on it. The kind of money that Miss Parsons could have spent but did not.

She went from the glittering world of Grosvenor Square to the squalor of a lovely but ruined home in Suffolk and death over a debt that meant nothing to her.

It was a sad end to such a promising start. Born ten years later and she would have been famous and revered in the engineering world. Instead she died a bitter old woman with barely a friend in the world. Yet another bizarre Suffolk tragedy.

8 Taylor

Murder in a Beauty Salon

The trouble for Maria Tonge was one that has bothered the human race since the beginning of time: two men were in love with her. She and John Taylor had had a relationship that lasted eight years. They had been engaged but he would not marry her. She broke off the relationship and then fell in love with Peter Davis. Taylor then wanted her and asked her to marry him.

It is a script played out in real life every day of every year. It is the subject of fiction and has been since man could write. It is the subject of plays back to Shakespeare and television shows the same story in various guises every night.

Maria's story had its finale in her beauty shop in Newmarket, the headquarters of British racing. The shops reflect this – there are specialists who sell saddles, whips and caps, covers for horses; blacksmiths; tailors who provide the gear for the gallops, and the right clothes for the meetings.

Houses are built with stabling to accommodate the horses and many are worth a great deal of money. The pubs and restaurants reflect the only thing worth talking about and on the ring of town are stud farms with their white painted fencing and immaculate hedgerows.

Maria was a beautician with a salon in Old Station Road.

If you passed her shop, the gallops were on the left and

if you continued up the road you ran alongside the great sweep of the heath where form is studied so assiduously.

She ran a good business and was popular with all her many clients.

It was her love life that was the problem.

Maria was an attractive, dark haired girl with a gentle disposition. She had an inner self which was attracted to religion, a boon to her after the traumatic events were over.

In the summer of 1977 her long relationship with John Taylor, who was a gun and firearms expert with a business in Lincoln, came to an end. They had been engaged but Maria finished it because he would not marry her.

She was one hundred miles away in Newmarket and it was in September that she met Peter Davis, an auctioneer who was nearly ten years older than her, and fell in love.

Peter, handsome and mature, lived just outside the racing town where he had his business. The couple got on famously and realized they were meant for each other.

Then Maria made a mistake. She wrote to Taylor to tell him that their relationship was totally finished. It brought Taylor racing down the Great North Road and across the fens to see her.

He was very upset and told her, 'He is not going to have you. I'm going to kill you,' but she did not take him seriously. He went back to Lincoln and she went out with Davis and continued to do so.

A month later she wrote to Taylor again to tell him that she had 'at last found true happiness'. It was a letter she should not have written. It brought a reaction from Taylor that she did not expect: he finally proposed marriage.

It was what she had wanted throughout the long relationship but now it was different. She was in love with Peter Davis and that surmounted everything she had felt for the guns expert in Lincoln. That flame had burnt out and was extinguished forever.

But only in her eyes. Not in Taylor's. He got in his car

and headed south again on 24 October. He brought no gifts for the woman he loved. Instead in the car he carried a loaded Smith and Wesson revolver with eleven spare rounds.

In the beauty salon he confronted the girl.

Maria remembered every second of it and she told it to the jury at Norwich crown court over six months later when two of the triangle were present. She spoke very emphatically and sincerely and appeared to still be in shock for what she had to tell was a truly horrible story.

Taylor came into the salon with a bag and began to talk. Maria said:

'He said "I was going to kill you as soon as I came through the door but after looking at you I could not." '

He went on talking and she joined in. He seemed to have calmed down, she said, but became upset again when she started to prepare a meal for the new love in her life, Peter.

She said, 'He broke down and said "There's nothing to live for. I don't care about my firearms and antiques but he is not going to have you." '

And that is when the conversation and events changed gear.

Taylor took his revolver out of his bag, put it to his head saying he was going to end it all but Maria managed to stop him – 'I grabbed it and he told me I had better put it down because it was loaded. I did. He put the gun down and they were just about to start talking again, she to try and explain rationally why he should not do such a thing, when Peter Davis arrived.

In a thriller it would be a moment of supreme drama to make the audience catch their breaths in anticipation of what would come next.

In the salon in Newmarket it was the worst possible moment, the worst thing that could possibly happen. It is conjecture but it might well have been that Maria could have persuaded Taylor to put his revolver away, have a drink and then go back to Lincoln, the raging fire of jealousy dampened down.

Instead the man he saw as his rival in love for the hand of Maria walked in and treated him in a matter-of-fact way.

Maria remembered it in exact detail when she had to describe it to the jury.

Taylor accused Davis at once. 'You have taken my girlfriend,' he said.

Davis said, 'I have done nothing of the sort. I am not involved in this. I would never take her from you if I believed she was in love with you.'

Maria said that she then spoke. 'Peter has nothing to do with this. I had decided to end the relationship before,' meaning before she met Peter. You can imagine the position she was in. She knew that Taylor had a gun, that he had wanted to shoot her and himself and that she had only just stopped him. She could not mention the gun because if she did, there was no knowing what Taylor would do. She just continued, as did Davis, to try and make the jealous ex-lover see sense.

Peter tried to reason with him. 'She's a very nice girl and I think she should be able to make up her own mind.'

Taylor said, 'I love her but I have not had any money to come down and see her.'

Davis took this in and replied, 'I quite understand the situation but I believe you had money for other things.'

He did not leave it at that, Maria said. Davis went on, facing Taylor, man to man in the room full of bottles and lotions, sweet smelling ointments and mirrors.

Davis said, 'As man to man I think eight years was a long time to keep the girl waiting. You should have known by this time if you loved her. You are a sensible man and my first impression of people is not usually wrong. All is fair in love and war.'

Taylor stared at him and then nodded. 'Well, I think I had better be going. Will you trust me to be sensible?' he asked.

Davis did trust him. It was a trust that was fatally misplaced.

It was no wonder that Maria could remember everything so clearly. For having heard the conversation which was as reasonable a discussion as could be held between two men who wanted the same girl, she kept her eyes on Taylor, expecting to see him leave the salon and go to his car and back north.

'But instead,' she said, 'he turned very sharply with a revolver in his hand. Instead of putting it in the bag and before I had time to think of anything, he shot Peter at a range of a few feet from the beauty room. I think there were six shots altogether. The first one I saw. I screamed to hide the gunshots. The third one ... I thought was for me.'

She went on, her voice slow and precise in the stillness of the court room, the man who had used the gun staring at her.

'Then with total fear, self-preservation came over me I'm afraid and I ran out of the shop.'

Davis staggered for his life the other way, out of the side of the salon into a passageway, pursued by Taylor, still firing. And when Davis fell Taylor stood over him and pumped the rest of the magazine into his body. He told police later, 'I didn't want to see him suffering. It's like game – I wanted to make a clean kill.'

Then he went to find Maria. She was hysterical and in a bad way. But Taylor was determined to have the last word.

He said, 'I did it for you. I killed him. I loved you.'

Mr Francis Irwin, prosecuting when the case came to trial in May 1978, told the jury:

'If ever there was an open and shut case of murder this is it. Obviously this man was acting under the effect of jealousy and jealousy is no defence to murder.'

Taylor denied murder but admitted firing the gun.

He gave evidence at the end of the prosecution case

which was over in the middle of the afternoon of the first day. He was not contesting the facts, just that it was not deliberate, cold blooded murder.

He said that he had gone to the shop and they had talked, all three of them. He went on:

'I went to leave the shop and at that moment everything just seemed to disappear. I can't remember any more at all. I felt something … I was helpless. The next thing I knew some shots were being fired. I was numbed in the mind and I felt almost it was being done for me.'

He was acting, he was saying, on remote control. He had a loaded revolver and it was firing through an outside force.

He went on. 'I can only say it was due to the tenseness of the situation. Mr Davis was not very forthcoming. I merely wanted to speak to him but it was very tense. It was very frightening and I can only say the tenseness of the situation culminated when I simply seemed to lose grip of everything. I cannot explain it.'

But it was an explanation. People do act as though someone else is controlling their actions. It was so with a Norfolk mother when killing her son. Her mind was full of cotton wool she said. She had been tried in the same court six years before for the murder of her young son, the fourth of her children to die. The first three died in accidents.

Taylor finished his main evidence and then the prosecutor, Mr Irwin, rose to question him. He did not have many questions but they were all to the point.

Yes, agreed Taylor, he was upset. Yes, he was jealous and upset at what he saw was the unscrupulous way that Davis had supplanted him and yes, he killed him for that.

And yes, when he fired those shots, he did intend to kill Davis.

The next day, before the trial continued, Taylor had a consultation with his legal team and when the court resumed he changed his plea to guilty. On the evidence it was the only thing he could do. He had no defence at all.

The judge, Mr Justice Griffiths, told him:

'If it is of any comfort to your peace of mind I now tell you that you made the right decision in changing your plea to guilty because on the evidence you had no defence whatever to the charge of murder.'

He then sentenced him to the mandatory term of life imprisonment but made no order as to the length of time he should serve.

Maria went back to her salon in Newmarket and closed it soon after. She had no wish to work in the place.

The story might have ended there but for a literary agent who came to see her about writing her life story. He was twenty years older than Maria, who had never slept with a man until she met Taylor at the age of twenty six.

She and her new love rejoiced in their newfound happiness, she a girl who had found sanctuary in a convent after Taylor was jailed, he a divorced man whose career included finding Martin Bormann, Hitler's lost deputy, allegedly working in a scrapyard in East Anglia.

It did not last and Maria went back to the convent and stayed.

The murder was in line with others in the area. Different.

9   Evans

Wife's Lesbian Affair

Thirty miles north across the fens is the town of March, once the administrative centre for both Hereward the Wake and the Isle of Ely county council. It has a famous church, St Wendreda's, which attracts visitors from all over the world to look at its roof. It was also the centre of the eastern counties rail network with the second largest marshalling yard in Europe. The Germans, who had the largest at Cologne, made several attempts to bomb it during World War Two but now it is a vast tract of windswept land with a prison built on it.

It is not a town that attracts much crime although it was the birthplace of one very evil man (see preface) and has had its fair share of domestic violence and robbery. But the oddest involved people who had come to the town.

In the summer of 1975 Lynne Evans (not her real name) was working at a hostel for the handicapped and it was there that she met Christine Nicholls (not her real name). Lynne was a year older than Christine at twenty-four and she was married to a Welsh school teacher Peter who was a year younger than his wife. They were happily married until Lynne met Christine.

They fell in love and slept together. That was how Peter found out. There was a love bite on his wife's neck when she came home to their house in March.

He taxed her, thinking it might be another man and was

shocked when she said that it was another woman. Worse, she told him that she didn't care what he thought and would not promise that it would not happen again.

Peter's bid to keep his wife was told when he appeared in the dock at Norwich crown court in February the next year.

It was, said Mr Justice Mars Jones, one time banjo-playing co-member of the Cambridge Footlights with Jimmy Edwards before World War Two, 'a truly terrible story.'

For after Lynne had told her husband about her affair with Christine, she made a suggestion that he reluctantly accepted.

Lynne, mother of a five-year-old son, was in no mood for a refusal in any case. Her husband told the police in a statement, 'My wife asked if Christine could come home with her and hinted that the three of us would sleep together. I agreed.'

Peter told the policeman taking down his statement, 'I thought perhaps I might be able to keep her once she came to her senses and realized what she was doing would not lead anywhere.'

Poor misguided, trusting fool.

It was doomed to failure from the start. He described it as a 'vile life' and it was.

He said that the first time he tried to make love to his wife's mistress he failed. Not surprisingly really. It was something that he did not want to do.

But he persisted and over the next month managed it. It was too much to bear and he told her not to come to his house again.

His wife played her next trump card, Peter went on in his statement:

'Both said that if I did not let them sleep together several nights a week they would telephone the school and smear my name over the affair which had been going on between the three of us.'

He knew that fair haired Lynne and her brunette lover meant it.

He gave in. 'I agreed because I valued my job highly,' he explained miserably.

So the lesbian affair moved on a stage.

'My wife only slept with me when she wanted a favour like Christine sleeping with her.'

On other nights the husband lay in one room, cuckolded in the next by his wife and her girlfriend making love.

It got worse as the two women went out on the town leaving him to babysit and then they returned, having had a few drinks, before stripping and making love to each other in the matrimonial bed while Peter lay in the spare room on his own, listening to what was going on.

He protested and in return his wife played her ace. As his despair became greater and as the nights grew longer he protested more vigorously. His wife told him she would leave with their son unless he stopped trying to part her and Christine.

It was all too much.

'I lay awake crying inside myself in the spare bedroom on my own.'

Finally his self-control snapped. The normally placid Welshman, popular with the children and staff, always cheerful, grabbed a kitchen knife and set about his naked wife, slashing her twenty times.

Her naked lover tried to intervene. Peter responded by stabbing her too. He plunged the knife nine times into her naked flesh and as she grasped her bleeding wounds, he got hold of her and did what he wanted to do for months.

He threw her literally out of the house – through the glass of the front door and left her bleeding on the path outside.

Provocation there had certainly been and it had been compounded by the threats of his pretty wife. What greater provocation could there be for a happily married young man than a wife to prefer a woman, to make love in their bed while he wept in the spare room, to threaten to expose the three-in-the-bed sex he had unwillingly gone through to try and keep the wife, and to threaten to take away the little son he loved if he did not stop attempting to end the very active lesbian affair?

But the law does not take such behaviour into account when a man takes a knife and wounds; slashing and plunging into bodies whether they be naked or clothed. The law takes a very serious view indeed as Peter found out when he pleaded guilty to wounding the two women.

They were not in court to hear the judge say it was a 'truly terrible story'. They were not living together but their affair was still going on he was told. It made no difference.

'Whatever the provocation such savage merciless attacks have to be punished,' he said.

He sent the school teacher to prison for three years.

In the eyes of the law it was a just sentence for such an attack. In the eyes of rational judges who hear stories of violence – but rarely so strange as this – as part of their daily working life, they know that it has to be stopped and the only way to stop it is by passing punishing and deterring sentences. They may well be right and probably take into account the fact that people like Peter might well do it again if they had the chance.

They may be wrong. To lock a trembling, frightened school teacher up for such a long time for trying desperately to save his marriage and keep the mother of their son at home, seems harsh and unnecessary.

10   Sparrow

An Eternal Triangle

Eye is one of those beautiful Suffolk towns like Lavenham and Hadleigh that half takes your breath away when you first see it. It snuggles on its own in the folds of the countryside and has a fifteenth century church and a timber-framed sixteenth century Guildhall amongst Georgian houses and the ruins of a castle. There are some wonderful carvings on the buildings and houses and it stands on the edge of Breckland and Norfolk. It has one famous son, the artist William Hoare, a contemporary of Gainsborough from Sudbury, and one of the earliest members of the Royal Academy, being elected in its second year in 1769.

It was also the setting for a crime of passion that matched anything Hardy could find in his native Dorset. It was a murder involving a deep brooding jealous farm worker and a pretty blonde who had married her farm worker employer. He had said that she could go to her lover if she wanted.

It was, said the prosecution, when the matter came to the old assizes court in the castle at Norwich, in September 1956, a drama of love, lust, drink and death. To which the defence countered that in the case of the killer it was encouraged love and betrayal.

Eileen Morley was a country girl who went into service when she was fifteen in 1942. She later went to work for

Frank Morley, ten years her senior, when he parted from his wife, and within a year, when 18, she discovered she was pregnant. They lived together and married a year later when he divorced his wife.

Three years before the drama, in 1953, Morley brought a friend home for a cup of tea. He was another farm worker, Victor Sparrow, a year older than her husband, and a bachelor. They all got on well and went for a drink in one of the pubs in Eye.

There was no love at first sight between the pretty fun-loving young woman and the serious, attractive Vic. It grew because she and her husband Frank began to quarrel over him staying out late drinking with his friends while she stayed at home looking after her son. She began to look for sympathy and found it with Vic.

In a statement to the police later he told how the affair started. He said:

'She wanted to go to Ipswich but instead we drove around in my car. We went to Riddlesworth Heath and we called and had a drink on the way home. She gave me the impression she was not happy at home and wanted me to get a caravan and take her away. She said, " 'I think the world of you and have never loved a man like I love you." I have got letters to prove this. After that I went with her two days and nights nearly every week without her going home. We used to spend the night in my car. She used to say to me, "Please get me somewhere to go with you because I hate living like this." '

He was 'intercoursing' with her four times a week and 'she would hang the curtains in a position so I would know when she was alone.'

'I started to sleep there chance nights and one morning when Morley was gone to milk she called me in and wanted me to go and get into her bed. I would not and she asked, "Shall I get into your bed then?" and I said, "No, the boy will talk and tell his father," but the boy said, "Get into mum's bed, Vic," and she said, "Come along, I am not worried you know," but I did not go. I dare say some men would.'

Eileen said later, much later, that she had no shame because she felt she was getting a raw deal from life and needed some compensation.

She was to get a very raw deal because in the height of passion she fell ill with tuberculosis and from June 1954 until September 1955 she was in hospital – thinking at first about Vic, the man to whom she had sworn her love. But while he did not visit her, her husband did, and encouraged her to get well.

They decided to try again with their marriage but when she was back in her regular haunts Vic came back into her life. Her husband now knew and there were two versions of what his reaction was.

At the trial Vic said that the husband had said to him, 'If you want her, take her.'

Eileen said that Vic gave her a letter to give Frank in which he wrote, 'If you don't want her I will take her,' and then later wrote, 'If you ever lay a hand on her it will be too bad. I will go through water or fire to see her happy.'

These were the words written by a farm worker, not in the fictional world of Dorset or Nottinghamshire, but in reality in the Suffolk countryside where things were very different to the way they are now. Electricity did not pump through the cables to light every house. Families sometimes could only watch television if they went into the pig sty where there was electricity. Running water and sewerage were not the norm.

This was not the figment of anyone's imagination. The triangle of Frank, Eileen and Vic was as real as it could be and the emotions that were being aroused and being expressed, whatever their limitations in education, were reaching a point where something frightful was going to happen.

It began to boil when Eileen decided to stay with Frank. To Vic who had bought a caravan as their home and described how he met her one day in Eye, – 'I picked her up like a painted doll. I thought I had got a rare capture' – it was a devastating blow to the solar plexus.

Eileen said at the trial, 'I told him that if at any time I became unhappy I would go away with him. At this time I told him I was happy with my husband and not to write to me any more. Once when I told him this he took my wedding ring and said he would have it as a keepsake.' Much later the police gave it back to her.

Vic did as he was asked. Whether he intended to do so forever is speculation but he kept away until April when he broke into their farm cottage but left soon after. Eileen did not meet him either, promising her husband that she would not betray him again provided he was good to her which he was. Eileen was to say later that she betrayed Vic but she was in a terrible dilemma: she had to choose her lover but give up her son or choose her husband and child. Both, she said, tugged at her heart strings and her maternal instinct won.

She wrote to Vic to say she was finished with him forever. In reply he told her never to go in the Horseshoe Inn. Perhaps it was because they had had a special meeting there and the thought of her there with another man, even if he was her husband, was too much for him.

On August Bank Holiday Monday, 1956, on their seventh wedding anniversary, Eileen went to the pub with her husband and some of their family. They drank and laughed and she ignored the warning that her jilted lover had given her.

Outside in the dark he stood, watching, with a revolver which he had bought at Bury St Edmunds market for three pounds, having been inside and seen her.

There was murder in his broken heart and he was ready to die too. He had nothing to live for without the woman he loved.

The real tragedy, far worse than anything in anyone's imagination, was to happen.

It was a lovely summer's night when Frank and Eileen stepped out into the sweet smell of the town. Eileen had seen Vic while in the pub. She said in the witness box, 'He was looking at me all the time in a dreadful way. He looked deathly white and bad tempered. My father went to get the car and we all decided to leave.'

Vic was already outside waiting.

'When I got near the car I turned round and saw him standing close to my husband. I saw him with a gun in his hand and I saw him do something to the top of it.

'My husband went towards him to get the gun but I could not see if he reached him. He pushed my husband back and shot him. I saw him fall and lay where he fell.'

She heard three shots. 'One hit me in the right arm. The third shot went through my handbag and my step-mother's dress. I took two strides into the middle of the road and lost consciousness and when I came to I was on the way to hospital.'

By passing out she missed the end of the story, the reason why it is included in this book. Vic did not know the difference between left and right.

He wanted to kill himself, thinking he had finished off both the woman he loved and the man who stood in the way of happiness. Two hundred yards from the pub he stopped and turned the gun on himself.

But he pointed to the wrong side of his chest. Instead of shooting himself through the heart on the left side he put the gun to his right side and fell badly wounded, but not, as he so clearly wanted – a note found at his home the next day said, 'Don't worry, I want my way. I am dying happy' – mortally.

He was taken to hospital and police kept a bedside watch until he began to recover and was charged with murder. He said, 'There is nothing more I can say.'

He appeared in court eighteen days after he had shot himself and was tried at Norwich in October.

The prosecutor told the jury after Vic had pleaded not

guilty to murder that, 'this is as clear a case of murder as you are ever likely to hear.'

It was, he said, the story of an eternal triangle but with a difference because the victim was the innocent husband.

The jury heard all about the affair, how she went to hospital, how it resumed after she came out and how it came to an end.

In a statement to the police Vic said, 'Her husband told me "Eileen says she thinks a lot of you and she doesn't want me. You'd better take her." '

He said that eventually he told Frank he was going to take his wife and 'he nearly went mad and she stood with me laughing and then I left.'

He later asked her for her wedding ring to prove that she would not break her promise to go away with him and live in the caravan he had bought. She did give him the ring but did not go.

He waited a week and then wrote to ask why she had led him on. She wrote back to say she had now settled down with her husband.

Vic told the police, and you can feel the bitterness with which he said it, 'It's all she's worth now but I wouldn't chance my life on a rotten woman like her.'

But he did. When he saw her in the pub the hatred grew and the despair he felt became overpowering. He told those that night when it became too much that he was 'looking for trouble' and he certainly found it.

Instead of finding heaven he found the dock and was facing the rope, for hanging was the penalty for murder then.

His counsel, Mr Lionel Jellinek, gave the jury an insight into what was in Vic's mind. Lowly farm worker he might be but he had passions and feelings that were only tapped by his love and lust for his friend's wife, encouraged by her and shared by her.

Mr Jellinek said that after months of emotional strain the sight of Eileen in the pub 'sent him round the bend'.

For he was an inadequate personality whose 'whole life was changed, was brightened by Mrs Morley. She gave meaning and purpose to his life. His whole thoughts and emotions were centred round her.

'She promised to go with him and gave him her wedding ring and when this wretched man had been worked up and got everything ready and was just waiting for the moment for her to come – on the very day – she changed her mind and said "I'm not coming".

'This inadequate personality was exposed to this terrific emotion. He was labouring under an emotion under which an even stronger man might have found it difficult to keep his balance.

'It is amazing that he shot Morley, the complacent Morley who had said, "if you want her, take her". He didn't want her. You may think he had not wanted her for a long while.'

It took the jury over three hours to find the sad, unhappy lover guilty of murder. There was only one sentence and the judge put on his black cap to tell him that he would be hanged by the neck until he was dead.

They took the man who did not know left from right but who could write vividly of his love and feelings, down to the cells and then to Norwich to await execution.

He knew there was a chance that he would be reprieved because a new hanging Bill was due before the House of Commons in November and might mean that the law would not take its course.

He was sentenced on 26 October and he had to wait until 12 November before he was told that he would not die (as he so wanted to but not that way) but would serve life imprisonment.

He started the interminable time behind bars at the age of thirty-nine with his memories of what might have been.

Frank, aged thirty-eight, was long dead but his widow, then twenty-eight, had to go back to her home town where most people cut her dead.

By January she was gone, married to another farm worker, a dairyman from the north of England, who was fourteen years older than her.

No one knows what Vic said or thought when he heard. Fiction can find a trite ending. Life cannot.

11   Pennington

Jealous Wife's Revenge

Suffolk has many market towns – small, friendly places where farmers and others from the countryside can come in one day a week to do business and have a drink. For these towns had all day market licences long before the new law which now allows all day opening at the publican's option. Sudbury is such a town, a bustling place with a population of over ten thousand, its native Suffolk people swelled a little by the London overspill plan which brought more people and industry back. Back because in the eighteenth century it was the largest of East Anglia's woollen centres and a busy port on the River Stour when its favourite son, Thomas Gainsborough, the painter, was born. That was in 1727 and at the age of fourteen he left to go to London to seek the fame and fortune which he found. The town still retains some of its earlier history. There is the medieval Anchor Inn and the fifteenth century Salters Hall and the Market Hill, the centre of the town.

American servicemen lived all round Suffolk and in other parts of East Anglia. There still are massive bases at Lakenheath and Mildenhall. American airmen and their families, officers and their wives often lived in the rural community in the Sixties and Seventies.

Among them were Jimmie and Willie May Pennington, a young couple from Indiana. Jimmie was twenty-four and an airman. His wife was twenty-three and at the time had a son called Bart who was fifteen months old and a new baby of five weeks, Dereck. They lived in a rented house in Station Road, Sudbury. Their marriage was stormy.

One Sunday afternoon in May 1960 Jimmie staggered out of their home, clutching his stomach and looking for a hospital. His drunken state must have put off those who saw him from offering help. It was a search that was to last a long time and in between looking for a hospital he was also looking for a taxi to take him to one. He had very little luck as he wandered through the streets, drunk and bemused – and losing blood very rapidly because he had been stabbed in the stomach.

It was eventually a race against time because he was bleeding so badly that if he did not get to a hospital soon he would run out of blood and be dead.

He lost the race. He finally reached a hospital which was at Bury St Edmunds, almost twenty miles away, because there was no hospital that could do anything for him at Sudbury, but it was far too late.

He was dead before he arrived.

Once the doctors saw the wound in his stomach they started enquiries and both the British and American Air Force police were involved. Both went to the house in Station Road, saw the hysterical wife, asked her some questions and then arrested her. She became even more hysterical when the Americans took her children away after they had put a piece of paper in front of her and she had signed it on their orders.

The next morning she appeared before the local magistrates and while still not understanding what was really happening, she was remanded in custody for a week and whisked up to London and into Holloway jail, the prison for women, until her next court appearance.

The British had her but the Americans had the children and also the body of her late husband. It was common thirty years ago for the Americans and the British to be involved in the same crime but for both to be working under quite different laws and systems. The Americans preferred to take into their custody any American who had committed a crime on British soil and put the person through their judicial process.

They did so in the case of Master Sergeant Marcus Marymont who poisoned his wife on American soil in the sense that they were in USAF married quarters on the enormous American base at Sculthorpe at the time. But when the crime was committed in quarters rented from the British but on English soil they were in difficulties. The year after Willie May's case they tried to have Willis Boshears transferred to their custody after he was arrested for the murder of a teenage English girl in Essex but the local magistrates would not agree. At the Essex assize court Boshears was eventually cleared of a murder on the grounds that he was asleep at the time.

The Americans had earlier faced the same problem over the terrified widow of their airman Pennington. They did not apply to try Willie May but they snatched her husband's body.

The first anyone knew of it was when she appeared on remand on 11 May. She was being defended by Dale Parkinson, a solicitor who practised locally but also had a thriving practice in London – he was later to be involved in the defence of the Rolling Stones – and was also a member of the American bar, unusual in those days. He was a well built, forceful man with a sense of humour.

After the prosecution had successfully made an application for her to be remanded in custody for a further week, Mr Parkinson rose to his feet. He said, 'I was amazed to be told last night by long distance calls from Indiana that the body was in fact in the United States. For reasons which I do not understand the coroner has released it and I cannot see it and nor can my medical advisers. My instructions are that the deceased did not die as the result of the wound at all.'

He said that he wished to protest strongly over the body being removed from the West Suffolk hospital at Bury St Edmunds and he also wished to protest equally strongly about the fact that Mrs Pennington had been forced by the Americans to give her consent for her children to be taken back to the States. That consent was now withdrawn.

As a result of Mr Parkinson's protests two things happened: the children stayed in Britain, looked after on the huge base at Mildenhall, just into Suffolk but in the fens.

The second thing was that the coroner explained why he had released the body to the Americans. He had, he said, no option under the Visiting Forces Act.

The next day Mr Parkinson made a successful application in the High Court for the two little Pennington boys to be made wards of court to stop the American Air Force authorities taking them out of the country. Their mother stayed in Holloway.

A week later, because justice moved very swiftly in the countryside in those days, Mrs Pennington was committed for trial by the magistrates at Sudbury. But this time she was granted bail in her own recognisance of £50 and on another surety from a chaplain at the base.

Mr Parkinson again did the trick. He told the magistrates that there had been 'horrible provocation' with a husband telling his wife, who had just come home after bearing him his child, that he was committing adultery with a local girl and that he had given her a ring.

It was no deliberate act with a knife, he said. The wife did not mean to kill him.

The local police sergeant, called to the house after Pennington had died, said, 'She handed me the knife and said "I did it. This is what you want. This is what I used." '

But later when told that her husband was dead and she was being arrested for murder she said, 'Oh my God no. I didn't mean to sir, please, I didn't mean to.'

After hearing part, but only part, of what happened, the

magistrates reduced the charge from one of murder to one of manslaughter, a much less serious crime.

This is what they heard from the prosecutor, a barrister from the Director of Public Prosecutions office.

He alleged that on the Sunday her husband was entertaining three men in their home and they were all drinking. Mrs Pennington was looking after her tiny son and the baby as best she could.

Then Pennington began singing a song to tease his wife.

'Standing on the corner, just around the corner,' he sang, strumming on a broomstick as though it was a guitar, 'watching Jasmine go by.'

Jasmine was his lover, a local girl of fifteen to whom he had given a ring which she showed off to friends, telling them she had been the six foot tall Negro's lover and loved him and always would.

It was the fact that she was coming round that afternoon with which he taunted his smaller wife. She reacted by throwing a bowl of boiling water in his face. There was violence and she grabbed a knife.

She was alleged to have shouted, 'I'm going to kill you, Pennington,' and the knife went into his stomach.

That was the provocation that the magistrates took into account. They added just one more condition to her bail – that she handed her passport to the British police.

It was a simple enough condition, one that is often imposed. But the American Air Force were not going to play ball. Instead of handing it over to Mr Parkinson, they refused. It was not just a matter of saying no, as Mrs Pennington had to remain in police custody until the passport was produced, but a declaration that they were not going to hand it over to a foreign power.

Mr Parkinson said, 'I literally had to fight all over again for her freedom. I rang Wethersfield air base and asked Colonel Reed for her passport. He refused to hand it over saying, "I won't hand over an American passport to a foreign government." '

The solicitor then threatened to take the matter to a higher level, bringing the Foreign Office into the dispute. That made the Americans think again and they said they would consult their Embassy. More time passed as Mrs Pennington waited in the cells at Sudbury. All she wanted to do was to get out and see her children who were now with a nurse at the base.

The way they had been taken was as high handed as what was going on. Mr Parkinson told the High Court:

'As soon as this girl was arrested, American officers pushed papers under her nose. She was so upset she signed them but she most definitely does not want her children to go.

'The truth is the Americans are acutely embarrassed because their paymaster won't pay for the children to be cared for. But if they won't pay for them to be looked after we most certainly will.'

And now, when it seemed certain that the children would be in her arms, the Americans were putting another obstacle in the way.

It is difficult to comprehend now, but it is only thirty years ago when the American attitude towards the British, on whose land they were based, could be perverse. On one occasion at Sculthorpe, just outside Fakenham in Norfolk, two electricians were marched off the base at gunpoint. The exact reason as to why the American authorities took this action against two British workmen was never given but the press officer on the base declared proudly, 'We'd do the same to the Queen of England in the same circumstances.' It was at Sculthorpe too that when a couple of their airmen busted the American Express on a public holiday they denied such a thing had happened even when the two started robbing off base. The Americans (compounded by Harold Macmillan and his government) denied flatly for five years that a sergeant had gone beserk and had held several people hostage for some hours while he pointed his revolver at a live nuclear war head. If he had fired the devastation in the immediate area would have been appalling. Reporters on the scene knew what had happened because Americans on the base who had been ordered to lie flat with windows opened and curtains pulled – just what you do in case of atomic attack – told them.

In this case hours passed before the Amerians finally relented and after discussing the matter at high level at the Embassy and with the Pentagon, they let her have her passport and she was released and reunited with her babies.

On 1 June, just a fortnight after the committal for trial, a very short time indeed by modern standards, Willie May Pennington, aged twenty-three, and a simple country girl denied manslaughter from the dock at Bury St Edmunds assizes court. Defending her was the up and coming Michael Havers, then with Leslie Boreham, now a High Court judge, one of the stars of the south eastern circuit. Havers, son of a judge and brother of the now Lord Justice Butler-Sloss, father of actor Nigel and former MP, Attorney General and Lord Chancellor, once appeared in the same court with his sister before their father, Mr Justice Havers, the only known occasion when such a family event has occurred.

In this case – described by the prosecutor as a 'very pathetic and sordid story' – he had a very strong and emotional defence to lay before the jury.

The violence in the Pennington marriage of just four years had not started on that Sunday afternoon in Sudbury. She had had trouble with his drinking and violence in the United States and had had an order made against him for his brutality. In Suffolk she had complained to both the American and British police about his behaviour and his heavy drinking.

On her return from hospital with her new baby she found hairpins in their bedroom. When she had complained she was assaulted.

The jury heard how on the Sunday, Pennington had three friends round and had sent one out to find some girls. He returned without success but the American told his Willie May that his new love would be round soon, Jasmine from the store on the corner, a girl of fifteen to whom he had made love and given a ring. A girl who told one of his friends after his death that she loved him and always would.

As the party went on and the drinking increased the Penningtons rowed as he taunted her about the girlfriend, strumming his make believe guitar as he sang of her and asking their fourteen-month-old son Bart, 'Have you met your stepmother yet? I have met my true love round the corner, the girl who works in the store.'

That was too much for his wife who went into the kitchen, grabbed the boiling sterilized water for the baby's bottle and hurled it in her husband's face.

The mood of the moment was revealed by one of the other men, two of whom were British. He was asked by Michael Havers, 'His behaviour was literally driving his wife mad, was not it?'

'Definitely yes.'

When Willie May threw the scalding water into her husband's face he retaliated by smashing her in the face so hard that her nose began to bleed as she fell on the floor.

In a quiet and soft voice, shivering with nerves as she spoke, Willie May told the Suffolk jury what happened when she picked up the long tapering kitchen knife with an eight inch blade for her protection.

She said, 'When I picked up the knife I was knocked down by my husband. Then the other three boys and my husband all had me on the floor. They were holding me and he jumped up and ran out of the kitchen. I did not know if he was going to get anything to hurt me because the others were holding me.

'I do not know how I got away from them– he was drinking and I did not know what he was going to do to my baby who was in the pram in the front room.

'When I went into the front room he grabbed me. He was between the pram and the door. I suppose I still had the knife in my hand. He just grabbed me to him and said "you have cut me".'

'He pushed me away and ran out. I did not know I had cut him. I rang the police to come and arrest him because we were fighting.'

Mr Havers gently asked her what she meant to do with the knife. She said she grabbed it to scare him because she was scared and had no intention of using it. The wound was an accident and she did not even know he was hurt.

Hurt he was although not fatally so, the jury heard. If he had got to hospital earlier and if a surgeon had been there, his life would have been saved. The wound, although deep, was not fatal in itself if he had been treated. But the time it took for him to walk about, finally go to a neighbour's house, finally be taken by ambulance nearly twenty miles to hospital in Bury St Edmunds was too long and he died. The speed at which police cars, ambulances and other services travel depends on how quickly someone alerts them. They are not always on hand as they are on television and however fast you travel if there are twenty miles to be covered, it takes time.

But he died and she was tried. When they had heard all the evidence – the provocation, the unfaithfulness, the taunting of a woman who had just had a baby, the behaviour of his friends who took to their heels after the stabbing, the violence of a husband who punched her and also hit her with the stiletto heel of her shoe – they also had Mr Havers telling them that she was a very frightened woman.

'She was up against a six foot tall fighting-fit Negro in a fighting temper who had had far too much to drink.'

The jury looked at the slight woman in the dock and retired.

They were back just nine minutes later, far less time

than they needed to have a cup of tea or cigarette, and the foreman announced their verdict.

'Not guilty.'

As tears ran down her face the court burst into applause with people clapping and everyone smiling. Outside the court strangers rushed to embrace and kiss Willie May and there was a feeling that justice had been done for the frightened girl from America who had been caught up in a foreign land where she did not know the people and the customs.

She said that all she wanted was to go home with her children, back to her home town, back to her parents.

Two days later she had her wish. The High Court returned her children to her.

12   Naggers

Victims of Nagging Hit Back

Naggers come in all shapes and sizes. There is no particular look nor class to a nagger. Some are born with cruel tongues that go on and on remorselessly, never ending their diatribe, others grow into it because the partner becomes slothful or apathetic. Some become naggers when the children go and find that years of constant 'do this' and 'do that' has become a habit. Some women do it during PMT or the menopause and in Suffolk a wealthy businessman strangled his wife during one such never-ending monologue. In Hampshire an accountant strangled his beloved during a PMT outburst when she took a stiletto heel to him while he was driving. He put out his arm to protect himself and save them from crashing, and throttled her. The police drew alongside as she slumped into the passenger seat and he told them all was well. He drove home to try and kill himself beside his fiancée's body but failed and landed up at Winchester assizes court where the jury acquitted him.

This story is about two cases of nagging that led to death; two couples from either end of the social scale, two partners who snapped for quite different reasons and in quite different circumstances.

In one case it was the wife who died at the hands of her husband and the reason for the nagging was the familiar one: no job, no money, and they were about to be turned out of home with two tiny children.

In the other it was the husband who died, a wealthy farmer who taunted his wife about her religious beliefs when he was drunk.

He was Gordon, aged fifty-two and known as Sonny. His wife was Joan, a church warden, aged fifty, and they had been married for twenty-six years.

As the years rolled by her husband drank more, became lazy, and parts of the farm were sold and there were continuous rows. She began to drink too and was on the verge of alcoholism until she became a church warden in 1960, twelve years before the killing.

Her husband used to taunt her about her religious beliefs which distressed her greatly and his drinking became worse. In April 1972 she was so upset during one row that she threatened him with a gun and called the police. When they arrived she was sobbing bitterly and asked them to take all the guns out of the house.

Her husband's drink bill was around £15 a week and when she appeared at Ipswich crown court in November 1972 – where she pleaded not guilty to murder on 29 August – Mr Roger Frisby, QC, prosecuting said:

'An incident arose which showed that the idea of killing her husband was in her mind. She told the two constables to take away the guns "or I'll shoot my husband".'

The rows became worse and in August much worse. Sonny was taunting her non-stop and on 28 August they had row after row at their cottage in Semer, near Hadleigh.

The next day she followed him and saw him go to a pub and then come home. They had a great row over cutting the lawn and she snapped.

She told the jury at Ipswich:

'I said to myself, "My God, how can I stop him talking like that," and then I saw this hammer. Something then snapped.

'I lifted the hammer in my left hand and as I lifted it he turned his head to me and said, "Joan, don't."

'As he said it I was bringing it down. I brought it down on top of his head as hard as ever I did. Once I had hit him I couldn't stop. I just kept on hitting him, hitting him. I don't know how many times. I can't remember seeing any blood. Eventually I threw the hammer down and ran to the phone.'

Behind her she left a blood bath. The blood was everywhere, on the seats, the sofa, the curtains and walls.

She rang her friend, the rector, who knew of their matrimonial problems, and he came straight over.

When he and Joan went into the study they found 'an appalling sight', said Mr Frisby. There was blood almost everywhere but Sonny was still sitting in his armchair and was still alive despite a double fracture of the skull.

He was taken to hospital but did not die for four days, so strong was his skull against the frenzied attack with the heavy hammer.

His widow told the jury, 'I cannot remember very much more about that day. I wanted to stop him from talking, from his everlasting getting on at me. I never thought about hitting him, that's the extraordinary thing.

'I was fed up with his tongue.'

Mr William Howard, QC, defending Joan, suggested to her doctor that she had been taunted beyond endurance and could no longer stand it. The doctor agreed. He said that Joan had told him that on the day of the attack her husband, who had been breathalysed the day before, had nagged on at her all morning after drinking and she wanted to stop him talking.

Her psychiatrist said that she told him they had rowed over cutting the lawn and when she started hitting him with a hammer she could not stop.

And her friend the rector said she was held in respect and affection by the local people and he knew how upset she became with the taunts by her husband over her religious beliefs.

It took the jury over three hours to find her guilty of

manslaughter and not guilty of murder.

She was jailed for four years by Mr Justice Boreham, son of a former senior Suffolk policeman who had been acting chief constable of East Suffolk for a while, who told her after hearing Mr Howard say there had been 'intolerable provocation' and 'agony of the spirit' that, 'The jury has come to a merciful decision in reducing the charge.

'You are described as, and properly described as, basically a good woman and I have no doubt that you have gone through a dreadful ordeal both at the time of the offence and since.'

Across the county Fred Jones and his pretty, outgoing wife Valerie (not their real names) lived in a tied cottage at Little Bradley in West Suffolk with their two daughters Rachel and Clare.

Fred was a farm worker who liked to stay in at night. His wife, dark-haired and attractive, liked the bright lights, dancing and having a drink. When they lived in Ipswich – and the reason for moving into the depths of the countryside near Haverhill – she became friendly with an American sergeant called Joe.

One night in 1969 she told her husband that she loved Joe and was going to live with him. They both said that there was a relationship but so far no affair. Fred and his wife talked it over and for the children's sake she made the great sacrifice of ending her friendship with the man she loved and going back to her husband. In a way it signed her death warrant.

She was true to her word and never saw Joe again. But there were rows in the tied cottage, so different from the warden's home although the rows were on the same pitch. In the rages and screaming matches that occurred in the tiny kitchen Valerie hurled pots and pans.

Then Fred lost his job which meant that they would have to leave the cottage which came with the job. She taunted him without mercy about his inability to provide for the family, the lack of money and the fact that he had no job. Despair and unhappiness has to come out in some form.

In March 1972 Fred went to the police to tell them that Valerie had left him to go off with an American airman she had met. She had abandoned him and the two little girls and he did not know where she was and could they help find her because the children wanted their mummy back.

His story was supported by a witness who said that she had seen Valerie walking up to the bus stop with two suitcases.

His story touched the heart of news editors on local papers and television and even made paragraphs in national papers. Her family were surprised and then perplexed that she should depart without a word to them and even more concerned because she did not make any attempt to keep in touch.

The weeks passed and there was no sign of Valerie, no word from her, not a phone call or letter. In May the police put out a press statement repeating the description and earlier information they had given and asking for anyone who knew where she was to come forward. A spokesman said, 'We are very worried about this woman's disappearance.'

Her husband stayed in the tied cottage as the date on which he had to quit came closer and closer, looking after the girls and trying to find a job. He had no luck so in the autumn he moved his family to Ipswich where he found work as a painter and decorator.

The new tenants moved into the tied cottage and in mid-November their black mongrel, Rummy, on a length of rope from the kitchen to give him room to roam, suddenly began digging in a vegetable patch near the kitchen window and the mystery of Valerie's disappearance was solved.

Police arrived and first they took out the jawbone that the dog had found and then the rest of the body. It was wrapped in a bedspread with the knees tied together and a kitchen towel round her neck with the knot at the back still in place. The post mortem showed that the towel had been used to strangle her and she was identified, even though it was obvious who she was, by matching her dental charts.

The police then went round to Fred's new home in Ipswich and asked him to accompany them to the police station to help them with their inquiries. He had been expecting them for eight months, ever since the day he had reported Valerie missing. He said, 'I thought she would be discovered sooner or later.'

He was tried at Ipswich crown court in February 1973 where he denied murder but admitted manslaughter. The prosecutor described him as 'cold a fish as you could see' but that was not how others saw him. A consultant psychiatrist said he was emotionally blunted and would normally walk away to avoid confrontation but the culminating effect of provocation reached a flashpoint with his wife and 'this was something which boiled up'.

Fred told the jury about her relationship with Joe which had ended three years earlier, about the rows over money and his inability to provide, all leading up to the morning when they fought over the kitchen sink.

Fred said there was an argument over having to leave the cottage. He said he remembered very little of what happened but, 'I know I had the towel in my hand. The next thing I knew I must have put it round her neck.'

The next thing he knew he said was that she was on the floor and she was dead. He panicked and took her upstairs and in the evening dug a grave and buried her in the garden.

He said, 'I had no intention of killing her', and then in the phrase that so many who are nagged use, 'I just wanted to stop her shouting.'

He was able to go on living in the house with his wife's burial spot outside the kitchen window and always in view because he had the two girls to look after and 'I just tried not to think about it.' It was not easy because he had to drink heavily to sleep.

Mr Thomas Field-Fisher, QC, defending Fred, said it happened because his wife taunted him about his inability to provide for her and her children and he was completely overcome by 'a momentary rage'.

The jury found him guilty of manslaughter, which he had admitted, and the judge, Mr Justice Melford Stevenson, not one who suffered psychiatrists gladly, said he took into account what this one had said and cut his sentence from the one had originally planned to eight years. He said to the hen-pecked killer: 'You are guilty of this most horrifying violence to this young woman.' It silenced her tongue.

13   Adams

The Hidden Mother

When David Stokes opened the prosecution case to the jury in the matter of Bill Adams (not his real name) a former officer with the Palestine police, he said, 'It is said that there are many strange stories about the fens. This is one of the strangest of all.'

It was. For thirteen years he pretended that his mother was alive and continued to draw her pension even though he had a fortune bordering on half a million pounds through stock market deals.

It happened in the small market town of Littleport, a fen town if ever there is one. It stands on the A1O between Ely and Downham Market with the River Ouse flowing at the back of it on its way down to Kings Lynn, The Wash and the North Sea.

To the east is Brandon across the fen and Thetford and Norfolk. To the north is Welney and the lowest land in Britain, six feet below sea level. Out on the road to Welney and its bird sanctuary and high banks reminiscent of Holland, are fields of gold black earth and the people who farm it, whether as the boss or the worker. The winds blow cold across the fens there, even colder than other places, and in winter there is little to recommend it except the warmth of the houses and the village pubs where no one is turned away. Sir Harry Legge-Bourke, old Etonian and guards officer, was the local Tory MP for that area for many years, a man you would not expect to meet in a fen village pub. But the fen men love an MP who is slightly different – when Sir Harry died they replaced him with Clement Freud – and they took Sir Harry to their hearts. He was chairman of the 1922 Committee and lived in Knightsbridge but he was just as much at home on the Welney Road in the pub with the rum old boys and tigers as he was with the best in the land over a glass of whisky or wine. He enjoyed a pint with the lads and they with him.

Not much has happened in Littleport over the centuries. It is the kind of place which people drive through but it has a stark beauty as you look across the fen lit by the last rays of the sun. The heat of the day oozes out of the soil and creates a thin web of silvery mist and the air is full of a freshness that no laboratory can match.

It was back to this place that Bill came in the late 1940s after service in Palestine with the police. What happened out there affected him for the rest of his life. He, was no longer the smart young man, the snappy dresser people remembered. He had been involved in the anti-terrorist activities and given evidence against the Stern gang who had placed him on their hit list. Friends said that the experience frightened him so badly that his nerves went and when he returned to the fens he became outwardly a strange and scruffy person, pointed out as a bit of an eccentric who hoarded things like a magpie, behaved like a tramp and lived in squalor, existing on tea, bread and tinned peas.

It was with this background that he lived until 1972 when something even more odd happened in his life but no one knew about it. Not until the end of 1984.

His parents were well off. His father William had a butcher's shop in the main street and owned several small farms and houses. In 1968 he emigrated to America to be with their only daughter Jessica to whom, when he died, he apparently planned to leave his fortune. After he left, his wife Eliza began to go downhill. Her mental health began to deteriorate and the power of attorney over her stocks and shares was given to her son, Bill, he of the scruffy raincoat tied round the middle with string.

Bill might be living in squalor but he had picked up one good trick from the Jews when he served in Palestine: how to wheel and deal in shares. Bill increased the family fortune to an amazing figure over the years.

By 1972 one of his mother's great friends died and after that she became increasingly senile so that by 1974 her two sons, Bill and Edward, were advised by their doctor that they should think about having her transferred to the psychiatric hospital at Fulbourn near Cambridge. An appointment was fixed for the psychiatrist to visit her but on the day he was due to come she vanished and the doctor was told that she had gone to Wisbech to be with a relative. In fact she was at another address.

In November that year Edward came home and found she was dead. He undressed, washed and laid out the body of the seventy-four year old woman and covered the body with a sheet. He was to say later that he did not see the need to call out a doctor at that time of night.

The next morning he went out to Prickwillow where his brother Bill was then living and told him their mother was dead but that he could not face the funeral and would leave everything to him. Edward left and the brothers did not meet for thirteen years and then only because the police began to investigate whether she was in fact dead – at the instigation of the Department of Health and Social Security.

It was to put Bill in the dock at Kings Lynn. And the jury listened in astonishment to the strange and grisly tale the prosecutor had to tell. Bill defended himself.

When Edward left in his distress he expected his mother to be given a Christian burial. She was not. Bill just closed the door of the bedroom in which she had died and left her there because he could not accept the fact that she was dead.

Two years after her death Bill let the house in Littleport to a young family who soon became conscious of a strange and unpleasant smell and could not help but notice that one room was permanently locked.

The husband mentioned it to Bill who said it could be the smell of bad meat that had been kept in the refrigerator. The husband then tried to force his way into the room but to no avail. He could see through the crack what he thought was a body lying on the bed. Bill immediately bricked the room up.

In 1979 Bill finally accepted that she was dead although his belief that she was not had not stopped him drawing her pension every week, an action that was eventually to be his downfall.

In 1979 he decided that she should be buried so he made an old wooden coffin and broke back into the bedroom and gently laid her in the box. He carried it outside in the dead of night and put it on the trailer of a tradesman's bike and pedalled through the lonely streets to where he was living in one room. He put the coffin in a shed and carried on living in the same way, eating frugally and amassing a fortune on the stock market.

Four years later the DHSS wrote to him to ask if his mother was still living with him. He said that she had gone to live with his brother Edward in Wisbech. The DHSS was not happy and eventually suspended her payment after Bill had said that he met his brother each month to hand over the pension money.

By that time the DHSS calculated Bill had drawn £9,343 pension that belonged to his mother. The might of the bureaucratic machine began to move and rumbled on. The police were called in and in March 1985 they went to see Bill.

He at first told them that Edward had taken his mother away but then said that she was dead and that he had been wrong to draw her pension. It was to help pay bills after a stock market crash in the 1970s.

But he assured them that her body was 'not under any floorboards or down any drains'. He took them to her resting place, a grave below a wall at the rear of the house to where he had moved and buried her because the shed was no longer a safe plce. Children played in there and rats were everywhere.

The coffin was dug up and a post mortem carried out. The pathologist found the mummified body of an old woman, dressed in night clothes, wrapped in a blanket and with her head on a pillow. She had died from natural causes.

When Bill stood in the dock he denied obstructing the coroner in the course of his duty and preventing the lawful and decent burial of a corpse between 31 October 1972 and 30 June 1980, by sealing his mother's body in the bedroom.

But he admitted obstructing the coroner in his duty and preventing the burial between 1 July 1980 and 22 March 1985 and to two specimen charges of obtaining money by deception from the Department of Health and Social Security.

The court heard that when the police first started questioning Bill he said he would not talk about it until he met his brother face to face and that is how they came to get back together. After talking, Bill talked to the police.

In his statement the old soldier said that he kept quiet about the death because he thought he might be accused of being responsible and worried about the family problems in America that might arise.

He told the jury that he used the pension money to maintain the family properties and to pay off debts. Some had been invested in shares to benefit members of the family.

Brother Edward gave evidence and said that when he told Bill that their mother was dead he did not seem to accept it and instead asked if she had made a will and began to discuss stocks and shares.

He had every reason to do so. When detectives started searching his tumbled down home looking for his mother they came across a gold mine.

For in the scruffy house they found shares, building society and bank accounts in Bill's name worth a staggering amount. The shares were worth over £350,000 and there was other money in trusts for his mother, brother, and his sister in America. In his own building society there was over £47,000. The total was over half a million and it staggered the judge, Judge John Binns, who described him as a magpie. It was an astonishing amount of money for any ordinary working man to accumulate.

For a Fen Tiger down on his luck and living in a manner that was difficult to understand it was incredible. But it has happened before. People who live in squalor sometimes do accumulate fortunes which they do not want nor spend.

Bill was one who lived to have it.

The police officer in charge of the case also told the judge that Bill was a normal person before he went to Palestine and his clash with the Stern terrorist gang obviously had a great effect on his life.

The judge remanded Bill in custody over Christmas for medical and psychiatric reports, delaying sentence for a month. The judge also wanted to think about what to do with this strange man although he did tell him, 'I'm thinking of a fairly substantial penalty.'

Bill expected a prison term as he settled in to a month inside Norwich prison. He found it not too bad. After a life of tea, bread and peas and a home little more than a hovel, a warm room with three meals a day was not something he was used to.

When he came back to court the judge read the reports. He learnt how Bill was seven stones lighter and phsyically and mentally unfit when he returned from Palestine and the dramatic effect his experiences really had had on him.

The reports made him change his mind. He decided it

was not necessary to send the old soldier to prison and instead fined him £7,500.

Bill had offered to pay back the pension money he had taken but there was a complication about this because he said that he had not deliberately set out to permanently deprive the DHSS of it.

Bill left court with his liberty.

He had made one firm decision in prison. In future he was going to be sociable and mix with people again.

14   Clarke

Debt Leads to Murder

On 16 January 1957, in the small and ancient assizes court at Huntingdon, Mr Justice Donovan, former Labour MP and now magnificent in red robes, reached for the black cap, put it on top of his wig adjusted it and then sentenced the young man in the dock to death. It was the last time this was to happen in this court where the sentence had been passed often over hundreds of years.

Then he added these chilling words:

'The circumstances of this case are so dreadful that you should not count on some other sentence being substituted.'

The young man shook with fear and apprehension and was taken from the dock to the cells and then to the condemned cell in Bedford prison where John Bunyan was once incarcerated and where, many years later, the A6 murderer James Hanratty was one of the last killers to be hanged in this country.

At the moment that the young man, a lorry driver, aged twenty-seven and married, was sentenced I was miles away on Farcet Fen, a Godforsaken part of the fens near Peterborough. I would rather have been in the court because it was the only time in my career that I would have had the chance to see the black cap used. It was not from any macabre wish to see a man sentenced swinging from the end of a rope but because it was part of English

141

history and tradition in our legal system.

However, it was not to be. I was the only reporter from my paper for the trial and only one other paper had just one reporter, so we pooled our resources against the might of the opposition, for it was a big story. A farmer had been brutally murdered out on the fen and the search and the manner of the killing and disposal of the body brought the national press down in force to follow the investigation led by Scotland Yard.

So there on that grim January night while the jury was out I was out on the fen heading through the dank mist towards Crowtree farm from where farmer Arthur Johnson's body had been taken in October 1956 after he had been killed.

It was an inhospitable area on a fine day but that night the black fields I could pick out in my headlights were menacing. The land lay slightly below sea level and it was bitterly cold. Some years later I was in the same general area but very late at night when a London-Edinburgh express crashed. It was a wild night with the wind howling and trying to find a phone box in the fen where roads run straight for miles and then turn at right angles with deep dykes and rivers to catch the unwary was difficult. Only the hardy live out there.

My colleague, Peter Stewart, who had sensibly decided to stay in the warmth of the court house and sent his younger companion to do the leg work, had reckoned that one of the other pressmen or even someone connected with the dead man or the killer might go to the farmhouse to just be there at the moment when the trial ended, ready for a phone call to give the verdict. Just why was not clear even through the mists of time, but people do these things.

Unfortunately neither another reporter, relative nor indeed a ghost was there. It was miserable, cold and eerie and after a while I went back to the court, only to find that the case was over, that the black cap had been used and the killer was on his way.

Peter filled me in with the details of the jury returning, the moment of drama and the reaction of the murderer. I told him about the atmosphere on the fen and he used it in his paper. It was not in mine.

Farmer Arthur Johnson vanished in mid October after returning from the pub. He was a popular local figure, a bachelor who liked a drink and a smoke and was known to carry large sums of money. He was not a tall man, but well-built and stocky.

On one thing everyone was agreed. He had no time for women. He would talk to them but was happy in the company of his male friends. He did have a woman in his house – his mother – and after her death various housekeepers, the last being Eileen Clarke, whose husband Morris was one of his employees on the farm. Two years before the murder they had moved into Peterborough, a few miles away, a cathedral city with engineering and brick making as its main industries, for Mr Clarke to set up a lorry business.

It was ten days before the farmer's body was found. The search began when there was no sign of him on the morning of 16 October when the men came to work. There were signs of blood near his house and the trail led to an outbuilding by which he normally kept his van, the vehicle he had used to go to the pub.

The van had gone but later in the day it was found out in the fen in such an isolated position that anyone not knowing the bleak landscape would have gone into a ditch or dyke. The ploughed fields, so wet and heavy that walking became very difficult after just a few steps, were traps as evil as any desert or quicksand.

The police were reasonably sure at the start that the killer would be a local man and when they found the van their suspicions were confirmed. There was talk, as there so often is, that the farmer carried a lot of money on him and it would be easy pickings for a thief. It was a case of elimination.

The inquiry was led by Detective Superintendent Wilfred Daws, known as Flaps because of the cockney rhyming slang, from Scotland Yard. As frogmen searched the icy, dirty waters of the dykes and other policemen with dogs covered the waste tract in freezing fog and damp, he made lists of suspects and organized the interviews and investigation.

He quickly knew that fingerprints found in the van were not those of the dead farmer but they did not match any held in the Criminal Record Office. He examined the dead man's wallet and in it lay a clue that he might have a girlfriend, which went against everthing known about him. It was a false trail but one name found in the wallet was that of his former housekeeper, Eileen Clarke, a pretty woman in her late twenties. She was interviewed and told how Mr Johnson was a quiet, generous man who had given a coat as a present for her daughter and how she and her sister used to go back and spend an evening with him after they had moved away. They played dominoes, a far cry from the rumours that wild parties used to go on there.

Ten days after he had vanished, a school teacher out fishing spotted a pair of feet sticking out of the water at Bevels Leam on Glassmoor Bank, an almost inaccessible spot three miles from the farm.

When the police pulled the body out, it was not a pretty sight. It was covered from head to waist with a sack and when that was removed there were savage blows to his forehead and back of the head with a cut on the neck. His skull was fractured and when the post mortem was carried out the pathologist found that his right leg was broken, suggesting that it had been run over.

The process of elimination of suspects had by that time come down to just a few and one was Morris Clarke who used to live at the farm. Police discovered that his lorry business was not doing well and that a cheque had bounced the day before the murder. It had been represented on Clarke's instructions that it would be met the day after the murder.

The police went to Clarke's home in Peterborough and searched the loft. In it they found sovereigns and a tin packed with notes, all of which came from Farmer Johnson's home. The thief had left the wrapper that went round the notes in the Farmhouse.

Clarke was charged with murder which he denied and came up for committal for trial at Old Fletton, just inside the county boundary. Mr Ryland Thomas told the magistrates, as he was allowed to then, what had happened. He was prosecuting on behalf of the Director of Public Prosecutions who, in such cases, sent one of his own men before the magistrates to lay the evidence that there was a case to answer at the assizes or quarter sessions courts.

He said that Farmer Johnson – 'It does not appear that he was particularly fond of the company of the opposite sex! – had had a few drinks at a pub with a friend and then went home. Next morning both he and his van were missing. In the house was an opened bottle of beer, the remains of a meal on the table and a bank note wrapper but no sign of the money. Ten days later his body was found.'

The prosecutor said that it would be extremely difficult for someone without local knowledge to negotiate the narrow tracks and deep ditches to the waterway at Glassmoor Bank where the body was thrown in. But if a person had that local knowledge he would also have been wary because of the danger of being bogged down in the newly turned potato field.

Clarke, he said, was a man with local but not recent knowledge. He and his wife lived at the farm for two years until 1954 while his wife was housekeeper. They left so he could set up a haulage service company which he did and operated unsuccessfully, running up large debts so that he had to sell his lorry. Then he got a job as a shunter driver.

The prosecutor said, 'He owed £600 to the Peterborough Engineering Company and £400 to another company for vehicle repairs.'

In 1956 these were enormous sums. You could buy a good small house and a car and still have a few pounds over. Debts of a thousand pounds were staggering for a man whose wage would not have been over ten pounds. It would be as big a millstone as a six figure mortgage is for a young couple now, except that they will always have some form of asset whereas Clarke had nothing.

Mr Thomas said, 'He gave a cheque for £200 to the other company in part payment and it was returned marked "return to drawer".'

Clarke did not have a bean but he told the company it would be all right if they represented it the next day – 16 October.

Just what he did during the late evening and early hours of 15/16 October were not known but the next morning he was down at the bank, shortly after it opened, to pay in £200 in cash and then went to see another creditor to whom he paid £34.

When he was seen Clarke said he had never been near the farm but suggested there had been an association between his wife and the farmer, a claim that was not backed by any evidence, Mr Thomas said.

But there was evidence of the money that was missing from the farm. In Clarke's loft was a bag containing five sovereigns, twenty-seven half sovereigns, £39 in silver, and an old-fashioned purse, identified by one of Mr Johnson's relatives as his.

There was also a small brown tin crammed with £642 in notes.

It was handed to one of the police officers when he gave evidence. Detective Inspector Charles Carrington sniffed it and said, 'It smells musty and damp, similar to the room where the safe is at the dead man's home.'

When Detective Superintendent Daws questioned

Clarke he said, 'It's Johnson's money and I killed him. I might as well tell you now.' He then made a statement which was admission that his act caused injuries to the dead man but it was not read at that court at the request of the defence. The magistrates were told that Clarke was pleading not guilty and reserved his defence.

How the killing happened was revealed a month later when Clarke stood in the tiny dock, rather like a small box at a theatre, in the assizes court in Huntingdon. The jury heard how the farmer was a generous man who 'kept himself to himself' while in company when it came to business matters but was a good companion. He had dropped a friend of thirty years off on his way home and the last words said were 'Cheerio, see you tomorrow.'

The morrow never came and Clarke told why when he came to give evidence.

The prosecution's view was 'that this man went to the farm knowing Johnson was in possession of money that he was going to steal and did not mind that in the process of stealing that money he had to do violence to the man who had been his employer'. The reason was clear – to get money to pay off his horrendous debts.

In his statement to the police Clarke denied that he had been near the farm on the night of the murder. He was in debt but no one was pressing him for money. He had sold his lorry and A-licence (needed to run his haulage business) for £920 and the £200 he put in the bank was his own savings.

He said, 'I have never quarrelled with Mr Johnson and we never saw any quantity of money in the house while we were there. He never talked about his business affairs to me.'

But it was a different story that Clarke told now. His wife was not in court to listen but earlier her mother had said there was no question of any relationship between her daughter and the farmer.

'I never suspected any relationship other than that of

master and maid while she was living there. I never heard any tittle-tattle.'

Clarke's version was different.

He said that for four years he had been jealous of the farmer and 'it had gnawed at his heart'. He thought there was a relationship but during the two years that he and his wife lived there, she assured him there was nothing and that made it all right. He accepted her word.

He admitted he was at the farm, having gone there late at night after a row with his wife. He wanted the truth: had there been an affair or not?

He went on: 'Johnson asked me to go into the house and talk it over but I said that there was nothing to talk over and that I just wanted to know the truth.

'I told him he had broken up my marriage.

'Then as I began to walk away Johnson got hold of me by the lapels of my jacket. I broke away from him and picked up a piece of wood from the ground. Johnson flew at me again and grabbed me by the jacket with both hands.

'I tried to get away but he flew at me and I hit him with the piece of wood. I hit him on the head. He went down but got up again and flew at me again. I hit him again on the head and he went down and never got up any more.'

Then he took the money as revenge.

The jury did not believe him. They had heard that after the killing his leg had been broken and he had been tossed like rubbish into the dyke, with injuries so bad that the prosecutor hesitated to show the photographs to them. They found Clarke guilty and it was then that the judge spoke:

'The circumstances of this case are so dreadful that you should not count on some other sentence being substituted for the one I am now about to pass upon you.'

So the lorry driver was taken to the condemned cell where there was nothing that he could do about his debts and where three clear Sundays would pass before he was hanged on the scaffold at Bedford.

But the judge was wrong. A year earlier the House of Commons voted to abolish the death penalty but the House of Lords rejected this. At the time Clarke was sentenced there was a proposal before the Commons that certain types of murder would still be punishable with the death penalty. Murder in the course of theft was one but because the proposal was still in front of the House, murderers were not being hanged.

He was sentenced on 16 January. On 4 February, just days before the gallows, he was reprieved and went to another prison to serve his life sentence. After a year he was allowed a pet and his family sent in one of his budgies to keep him company.

Two other things happened after the case. The farmer's will was published. He left £37,416, a vast sum in those days. And on the day Clarke should have hung the fifteen workers on a neighbouring farm to Crowtree were given the day off after the stock had been fed in protest against the reprieve. The farmer said, 'I did this because I believe that we can't have persons going about battering decent people to death and getting away with it. I feel that on the evidence that came out Clarke should not have been reprieved!

15   Tigers

Killing for the Wrong Loot

The murder of farmer John Auger, aged sixty-two, in March 1967, was the act of Fen Tigers behaving at their very worst. Tigers are hard working, decent men – rough and ready perhaps when compared with slick city folk – but basically hardy, good family men. But occasionally they can become fearsome criminals, but not using much guile as they do it. They plan things on face value without too much checking.

Mr Auger was a wealthy man with a magnificent collection of Staffordshire and Dresden china, antique chandeliers and clocks. He was adding to this with French furniture he bought at Sotheby's. His collection was well known amongst other collectors and the trade. It was worth something approaching a million pounds by today's standards. It was certainly one of the finest in East Anglia.

He had kept money in his home but prior to March he had had two attempted break-ins, but without success. After the second one in the autumn he said that he would not keep money in his house again.

The stories abounded about his wealth and what he had in the house however, which stood on its own by his 300 acres on the Wisbech road at Outwell, five miles from Wisbech, which dubs itself 'capital of the fens'. It was once a major port and although now eleven miles inland it is still busy. The Brinks, two rows of houses lining the River Nene, are some of the finest examples of Georgian architecture in England and it was the home town of Clarkson, the anti-slave trade campaigner.

The talk was that there was a fortune in the house and that the safe was bulging with notes and gold, and as the nights passed and the beer flowed, so the tales were exaggerated.

The tales sparked the interest of many and particularly three young men – local villains. They believed the rumours and so late one night set off, tooled up with housebreaking instruments and enough rope to tie up a ship.

What they did not know was that since the last attempted break-in where the raiders were chased off by the farmer and his dog, Mr Auger had changed all the locks and strengthened the doors of the four rooms in which he kept his china collection.

When they arrived the farmer was out for a late night walk with his dog before going to bed. He was a good farmer, a generous man, and well respected and liked. As he walked towards the dog's shed, the three pounced. One had a shotgun. They clubbed him unconscious and tied and gagged him, leaving him with mortal wounds to the head and tied up 'like an Egyptian mummy', it was said at their trial months later.

Then they went into the house and grabbed his wife, Isabella, aged fifty-nine, and tied her up too. They took a tablecloth and put it over her head to make sure she did not see what they were doing.

They told her,

'If you make a noise, we will shoot you.'

Then they got to work in the treasure house to take what they had come for – the safe which would provide them with riches. They found it and lugged it outside the yellow brick farmhouse. It was an old-fashioned safe, weighing four hundred-weight at least and it took some shifting. They finally got it on to the farmer's green Volkswagen pick-up truck and drove off. A neighbour saw it go but thought the farmer was behind the wheel. People did not think about armed robberies in the middle of the night in the fen in those days.

A short while later the Augers' daughter Audrey came home and found her mother in the house. She had fainted during the attack and after her daughter brought her round they armed themselves and went to look for Mr Auger.

They found him in a terrible state, his head covered with blood, outside the shed. He had been hammered to death with a two foot jemmy which had been found in the grounds. There was a fingerprint on it.

When the police arrived they found that the phone wires had been cut.

They also discovered that the thieves were as ignorant as they were violent and evil. They had taken the great safe which had not been opened for two years because the key had been lost. When they finally cut it open they found just two florins, twenty pence in today's coinage.

Behind, they left the collection of porcelain, china and antiques.

So who were these three men who had clubbed down the seventeen stone farmer so savagely that his skull had been split through to the brain?

The pride of Scotland Yard in the form of Detective Superintendent Wallace (known as Wally) Virgo arrived to lead the team which also included Detective Superintendent Reginald Lester, head of Norfolk CID, because although the crime was just over the border into Cambridgeshire, there was a suggestion that the killers might be from neighbouring Kings Lynn, ten miles or so away.

Virgo was a policeman of thirty years' experience who had been involved in several well-known murder inquiries including the Richmond towpath killing, and in the enquiry into the explosion of the Dara, a British ship that blew up in the Persian Gulf killing 200. After the Wisbech killing he went on to greater things and became head of the Flying Squad.

When he arrived in Wisbech he learnt several things quickly: that terrified local people had armed themselves with shotguns, coshes and large dogs, so great was their fear of housebreakers and thieves; that the three who had beaten the farmer to pulp were local men although they had pretended to be from London; and that three names were clearly in the frame.

Why the three were not arrested at once is difficult to fathom now but it may have been that the big man from the Yard, taken from his comfortable manor, wanted to do everything by the book instead of making a hasty arrest. It is however true that when national reporters arrived on the scene on the Sunday (and I was one of them) the local pressmen and local people named the killers. A young Cambridgeshire detective confirmed with a nod that the names we had were the names they had and they were itching to arrest.

Our newspaper stories made it clear that that was the position.

But Virgo took his time and it was well over a week before the three were arrested and brought before the magistrates. They were: Barrie C., twenty-five, leader of the crime, a well-known local thief who had done time for larceny and housebreaking but with no previous convictions for violence; David W., twenty-two, sometime painter and nightclub bouncer, a thief who had been sent to prison for turkey stealing; and Patrick C., twenty-eight, sometime painter, who had been to prison for house-breaking and had a string of convictions.

They all had different stories to tell the police. Barrie C. said from the start that he was not there and kept to his story right through to the moment the trial ended. Patrick C. admitted he was there 'but I did not use any violence'.

David W. said: 'I suppose somebody has squealed. I was there but you'll have a job to make this one stick. Even if you are from the Yard you won't prove anything. I was there but there was nothing left behind and you know it.'

The police did know it. They had left nothing there but there were other clues elsewhere and by putting them all together (particularly when the safe was found under a bramble bush by a dyke three miles from the farm), the police had a case.

David W. said one other thing to the police when he was arrested which was to become important at the trial. It was: 'I shall say you verballed me.'

The three came for committal at Terrington St Clement magistrates court and there was trouble with the prosecution's witnesses. Three were extremely reluctant to give evidence. A girl screamed hysterically in the waiting room and when she eventually went into court she and later the other two, both men were treated as hostile witnesses after they refused to confirm (or changed) the statements they had given to the police.

There was a great deal of fear among the local people who had to tell what they had seen and heard. The three had a bad reputation and one of the hostile witnesses was so scared that he did not turn up at the trial in Hertford.

But one exception to the air of apprehension was the farmer's widow. She told about her ordeal, how the men came in, how one threatened to shoot her if she made any noise, how she was trussed and gagged, how they pretended behind their stocking masks that they were from London, but she could tell they were local, how she heard the hiss of wheels as they moved the safe out, how one said 'We will have to take it with us but be quick.'

The men were sent for trial. Before they appeared at the assizes on 27 June, just over three months after the murder, the farmer's will had been published showing he left nearly £86,000 and his beloved terrier Patsy whom he was taking for a walk when he was killed, had been put down. She was very old and Mr Auger had been thinking of taking her to the vet to put her comfortably to sleep.

When the trial opened, the three pleaded not guilty and their defence was that all the police, the ten who gave evidence, were liars. The defence team consisted of three senior Queen's Counsel, two of whom are High Court judges now, who, as is the custom and procedure, accepted their clients' instructions to the letter. The fact it took the jury on 14 July just an hour and fifty minutes to find them guilty after a long trial shows what they thought of it.

The judge, Mr Justice Glyn-Jones, who had represented the parents after the Aberfan disaster, put the point to the jury in his summing up. He said that there was a black sheep in every profession but the defence was that all ten policemen who had given evidence, from detective superintendent to constable, were 'wicked police' who had all given fabricated evidence supported by perjury. Could that be so?

The case for the prosecution was that this 'ruthless, vicious attack' was well planned. They gave the farmer a terrible beating – 'demoniacal savagery', – and stole his safe which contained a couple of coins. Mr Owen Stable, QC, said: 'Had the robbers known that I doubt whether this horrifying crime would have been committed.'

As one of the three told the police, 'If only I could turn the clock back I would not have done what was done.'

But Mr Stable put it into perspective when he said in his opening address to the jury: 'Every now and again a crime is committed of such hideous proportions that even the most insensitive and hard-boiled person is made to sit up. Such a crime has come before us today.'

During the long days of evidence two points stand out: Virgo told the jury that crime had become so bad in Wisbech that people had armed themselves against it and one of the witnesses did not turn up.

He was one of the two men who had been treated as a hostile witness at the magistrates court and he had been warned that he should attend at Hertford. He had already been told that he would not be prosecuted if his evidence showed that he was involved in any crime. But he was so frightened that he did not turn up and the judge issued a warrant for his arrest.

When the trial was over the man was found and brought before the judge who sent him to prison for three months for contempt of court. The man said that he had been frightened and had been sent a letter. But he did not give the real reason to the judge. The police went to his home and twelve days later the man was again brought before the judge who heard that he had received several letters threatening violence if he gave evidence against the three killers. One, made up of words cut out of a newspaper, said: 'Don't do it on Tuesday. The only way is killing. Run fast, don't stop.'

That was enough for the man, who was to tell of certain times and places involving some of the killers.

The judge now accepted why he did not attend court to give evidence. He released him and said:

'I am satisfied you were intimidated. I believe you were not the only one in this case who was intimidated. It was foolish of you not to give me the real reason when you were first before me.

'This is not the first time that I have had wicked men who are charged with serious offences of which they are guilty, who will go to great lengths to intimidate witnesses. It could have been done by someone else acting on behalf of these three men because they were in custody at the time.

'Interference in the administration of justice is a grave crime.'

This happened almost a month after the end of the trial in which the three were convincted of manslaughter, not murder, because the jury considered that they had not intended to deliberately kill the farmer but did so in the course of their robbery.

The judge told them:

'This is one of the worst cases of manslaughter ever to come before me. The brutal treatment you gave to Mrs Auger illustrates the callous violence you were prepared to use.'

He sent Barrie C. to prison for fifteen years with these words:

'You were the planner of this enterprise. You are an habitual criminal and a grave menace to society.'

The judge gave the other two twelve years each and all three five years for breaking and entering the farmhouse and stealing the safe.

They were taken down and the judge made one more pronouncement before he left the court. It was to praise the police for their work, saying the jury had 'rightly and justly' rejected the allegations against them.

The defence the three killers ran was one that is less common now than it was. It was a favourite in cities but not often in country areas like the fens. It is simple: the police are liars. Recently, sadly, it has been shown that this was true in the case of the Guildford Four, the Birmingham Six and the Maguire Seven, which has stained their reputation far more greatly than the judiciary will acknowledge. When the Wisbech men used this defence it was a blanket defence, and the jury rejected it out of hand.

Would they do so quite so quickly now?

16 Doctors

The Doctors' Hiding Place

Two doctors met at a house in north London late on the afternoon of 14 January 1967. They had not got together to discuss medical matters but sex. They were both active homosexuals, moving in the twilight world in London where youths were available to be enjoyed and photographed. One of the doctors was deep into pornography and made plenty of money from selling his pictures in the Danish market.

Their partner in the practices that evening was a sixteen-year-old boy called Bernard who was slightly backward mentally and had been missing from his home in Muswell Hill for eleven days. He went to see the film *The Ten Commandments* and afterwards went to a local cafe with a sixteen-year-old shop assistant called Christine. He then wandered off, never to be seen by any of his friends nor family again.

Where he went during those eleven days will remain forever a mystery but it is almost certain that somehow he was lured into the evil world that existed then and still does today, where boys of his age go to amusement arcades and meet older and experienced men who are looking for victims to take part in sex orgies or indecent photographic sessions. It has been going on for years, not just in the West End of London, but in the suburbs and provinces. Sweet talking men can easily urge a boy to go to a party or for a drink. The drink can lead to drugs and then the boy is no longer in control of himself.

In recent years one such orgy degenerated into mass buggery and death as the victim, a lad barely in his teens, was suffocated spread-eagled over a stool as man after man ground into him, the full weight of their bodies crushing the life out of him. When he was found his face was tear-stained and the men were later jailed for long terms.

It is likely that young Bernard was somehow caught up with this web but what is certain is that he was in this house in north London and he was being used sexually. There may have been other men there but the doctors were the prime participants and their evening ended with the boy being strangled in a moment of passionate frenzy. They were left with the body. The first thing they decided was that it must be cut up for easier disposal. The problem facing the layman was not theirs. They had the skill and the tools to dissect the body in to as many parts as they wanted.

In the surgery where they worked, the atmosphere must have been that of the days of Burke and Hare. Under eerie lights they carved and cut the body on which they had lusted so fiercely a little while before into nine pieces. It was a macabre scene. Their sexual appetite and demand had put them in mortal danger of losing their liberty for many years to come. Their professional reputations would be ruined if anyone found out what they had done. Their world would come crashing down in the despair of a prison cell for just a few moments of gratification and satisfaction.

All this must have gone through their minds as they carved expertly. Just how long their gory task took is a matter of speculation. It may have been through the night, it may have been early Sunday morning because their orgy of death may not have ended until then. It certainly was no earlier than Saturday evening and no later than around nine o'clock on the Sunday morning, as confirmed by the pathologist. At first his face was clean shaven. The next day there was a growth of beard on the face. For a period of forty-eight hours after death the skin shrinks with lack of blood, giving an impression that the beard had grown after death.

Having finally cut the body up, the doctors had to dispose of it and had to decide where and how. They packed the pieces into two suitcases, one green, one brown and both cheap, and put the boy's jacket in too. They did not bother to remove the labels on one, nor initials on the other.

The obvious place to head from north London to find wide open spaces was East Anglia, a favourite dumping ground of killers (see *The Essex Triangle* and *The Norfolk Nightmare*) where the roads are straight and fast and not too busy at night. Whichever doctor did the gruesome task of dumping the cases, he headed down the A12 in a white transit van and at Tattingstone, just short of Ipswich, and just off the main road, he put the cases behind a hedge and hurried back home. Two vans were seen parked by the field at times during the evening of 15 January but have never been traced.

The cases were found soon after nine on the Monday morning by a tractor driver, harrowing the field. He had a look inside one and promptly called the police. To their astonishment there were the remains of a teenage boy, expertly carved up into nine pieces including his head.

Inside the first case with the head, was a jacket, which later turned out to be his, and a towel with the laundry mark QL42, and in the other was his arms, legs and other parts of his body.

On one case were the initials 'P.V.A.' in black letters which had been painted on and on the other were two shipping labels from the Union Castle Shipping Line on their Clan line which sailed from Britain to South Africa and the Middle East.

On one label was the initial 'R'. Inside the jacket was a matchbox label which was only obtainable in Israel and a receipt for an item of jewellery purchased in Muswell Hill. It had been given to a girl by the dead boy but he was not the person who bought it. He was never traced.

Suffolk police, newly formed in an amalgamation of Ipswich, east and west Suffolk, started the initial hunt into whom the dead youth was. Led by Detective Chief Superintendent Tom Tarling, head of the CID, they set up an incident room while Detective Chief Superintendet Harry Tappin came down from Scotland Yard. The Suffolk Chief Constable Peter Matthews automatically called in the Yard and Tappin arrived with his sergeant.

Lists of missing boys were checked in East Anglia but his description did not match any on the list. The search spread into London without results. The obvious way to identify the boy was to publish his photograph, an extremely tricky business because his face was in no condition to be shown to the public. The police therefore obtained the services of a mortician to clean up the face so it looked alive, open the eyes using glycerine, shave him, and comb his hair.

Newspapers printed the pictures and they were sent up to London. They appeared in the late editions of the London evening papers and you can imagine the shock that the dead boy's uncle had when he saw the face staring out at him on the front page.

He went to Tottenham Court Road police station, the family were told, and the father was driven down to Ipswich late in the evening to identify his son.

Once he had been identified the hunt for his killer split into two separate inquiries, one at Ipswich and run by Tom Tarling and the other in Highgate police station to follow the Muswell Hill connection run by Harry Tappin. It was the first time a murder enquiry had been run in this way and each day a squad from Ipswich went up to north London to work with a Scotland Yard team. They interviewed as many people as possible to try and fill the missing eleven days in the dead youth's life and also in the hope that they would find the killer.

As that operation moved into motion Suffolk police followed the clues that they had, the two old suitcases, the matches and the towel.

The towel had a laundry mark on it and the police established that it was made by a Polymark Mark 11B machine and the mark was QL42 on white tape. They went to the manufacturers who were not able to provide records of all the laundries they had supplied with the tape but gave enough names for the police to start asking.

As they asked they were given more names and by the time they had exhausted the list they had visited 640 laundries in this country and made further enquiries in Africa and the Middle East where the machines were used.

It was a painstaking job but sadly did not produce a result. The same result was unfortunately obtained with the initials PVA on one of the cases. Again working methodically the police traced over 800 people with those initials to try and find the owner. One woman claimed that they were those of her husband and she had given the cases away to a rag and bone man in south London some time before.

Then there were the shipping labels. On one it was clear that the surname began with the letter 'R' and a team of officers drove from Ipswich to the shipping offices at Southampton which was then a thriving passenger liner port. It still retains its rating as the busiest in Britain with the QE2 and Canberra but traffic now is that of a quiet country lane instead of the motorway of the seas.

The labels came into service in 1949 and police made a list of all those whose surname began with 'R' who had travelled on the Clan line. There were hundreds of them and it was an uphill and losing battle because it was clear from early on that many had left the country or had died.

But some of the enquiries did provide positive leads. One was that Bernard had last been seen with a man in a yellow Ford Cortina. Another was the two transit vans seen around Tattingstone. Tremendous effort went into tracing the three vehicles but again without success.

In Suffolk house-to-house enquiries went on in the area around Tattingstone, on the Shotley peninsular and in certain areas of Ipswich. Police particularly checked all known homosexuals. Tales that sailors held gay parties in houses in the countryside were also followed up but again with no success.

It was obvious to the two men leading the investigation that the killer was probably in the Muswell Hill or North London area and that he was a medical man or a man who had been taught anatomy and was homosexual. It took them into a world hidden from public view most of the time. It took them to clubs and pubs where such men picked up their partners. It took them to houses and flats where parties were supposed to be held, where other men might put them onto someone who could put them on to someone else who in turn had a name of someone with the kind of skills they were seeking.

It led them to two doctors. One denied any knowledge and had an alibi and was partly eliminated from the enquiry. The police were not sure. The other had gone from his home and haunts and was traced to South Africa where he was convicted for sex crimes some years later. There was some doubt as to whether he was in the Muswell Hill area the weekend on which Bernard was killed in some kind of orgy but when that confusion was sorted out he had gone. His description was circulated some time later to all police forces but he was never interviewed. In those days no police force had the funds to send officers to a country like South Africa to interview a potential suspect against whom there was nothing but circumstantial evidence and a feeling that he was responsible.

More and more people were interviewed – over 100,000 people of different ages, sex and behaviour – and eliminated. One committed suicide but that was because police had evidence of other sexual crimes and he faced imprisonment and disgrace. He was not the man who killed Bernard.

Time went on and the number of policemen involved in the investigation was reduced.

There were various theories considered. There was the possibility that Bernard, who worked in a warehouse, might have been tricked into going to the Ipswich area and there taken part in some of the orgies that were said to go on there at drug parties. The thought of going to the country might have attracted him. He was an animal lover with a white poodle called Pepe and a canary. They were of far more interest to him than girls. Police considered this idea for some time but it did not seem to make as much sense as the Muswell Hill killing and then dumping. That was pursued hard.

Both doctors who were involved in gay sex rings were spotted as potential killers from the moment their names were known. The first, Dr X, was a known homosexual, keen on young boys with a reputation for picking them up.

Due to paperwork confusion it was initially thought that he was out of the country when Bernard was killed and dismembered. Later it turned out that he was in fact in north London that weekend. By then he had gone to Africa and later went on to Australia and all trace of him has now (1993) vanished. Police know he had a conviction for sex offences in Australia and went to prison but once he was released they lost track of him. He would now be in his sixties.

In July 1967 an inquest jury returned a verdict that Bernard had been murdered by a person or persons unknown and he had died from manual strangulation. The formal verdict was nearer the truth than many suspected for the police thought that more than one person was involved in the killing. It is also a fact that if the killers had been caught they might have well argued in their defence that the youth died during sex and therefore he was not murdered but died accidentally which would have reduced the charge to manslaughter and carried a possibly lighter sentence.

In the winter of 1967 two suicides attracted the murder squad's attention. The first was in the Highgate area where a club receptionist and homosexual, aged thirty-three, died of a massive overdose of drugs. When the inquest was opened in St Pancras coroner's court in November his doctor said that the man had made two suicide attempts after he had been interviewed over the murder of the youth. The doctor said his patient, a psychopath who had developed a form of epilepsy, became extremely disturbed after the first interview and after the second, made an attempt to kill himself. His successful attempt followed soon after, after a row with a friend.

When the full inquest was held in December, police denied they had persecuted the dead man by interviewing him without his doctor being present and the coroner heard that the interviews had taken place many months before, in February.

The coroner recorded a verdict that the receptionist had killed himself and said: 'He was a man who was completely dependant on drugs.'

The other death was in Blackpool and came after a sordid party during which one man died. Another man at the party, Mr 'A', a clerk, aged fifty-four, poisoned himself in a cell at the police station. His initials included a 'P' and 'A', the same as those on one of the suitcases and he was a notorious gay who drugged his victims.

The inquest was held in November and the jury heard about the party in a flat on South Parade near the famous tower. During it one of the guests died in very strange circumstances.

He was one of a trio – Mr 'A' was another – who had been drinking in the Tower Bar. The third man said in evidence that the next thing he remembered was feeling drowsy and then he recalled being blindfolded and being held on a bed and someone pushing tablets into his mouth. That tied in with other evidence that in three of Mr 'A' 's last five convictions he had given chloroform or drugs in drink to men before assaulting them.

The third man made one clear statement. He said that he did not take part in the murder.

The jury agreed. They returned an open verdict on Mr 'A' but said that they had come to the conclusion that he was the murderer.

What interested the Suffolk police was the way that Mr 'A' operated with drugs and chloroform. It might well have been the way that Bernard was treated before the assault on him. Suffolk and Lancashire police both worked on a possible link but eventually decided there was not one.

The next clue came four years later when one of the Sunday papers reran a story about the case which refreshed people's memories. One of their readers, a widow in her sixties, recognized the suitcase with the initial 'R' on the label and remembered it as hers when she saw the initials 'PVA' on it. She said that she had sold it to a Steptoe in the Clapham area some years before. He was touting for business on his horse and cart around the streets. Police followed the lead but never found the man who had bought it and therefore were unable to find out to whom he sold it.

But early in 1975 the police had a genuine breakthrough. A London doctor called John, aged forty-one, committed suicide in his room in the Prince of Wales hotel, Proserpine in north Queensland.

He had practised in Muswell Hill, was known as a homosexual and had been interviewed and eliminated through lack of evidence in the initial enquiry in 1967.

During his medical career in London he had had practices in South Kensington and then, after north London, moved south of the river. It was there that he had been luring boys to his home, filling them with drink and then taking filthy pictures of them which were sold in Denmark. He also had sex with as many as possible.

He fled to Australia in October 1974, a few hours before police arrived to arrest him. He went to Bromley to say goodbye to his elderly mother and then flew to Melbourne. He was arrested there and allowed bail to appear in court on 27 December to face extradition proceedings but disappeared.

In the gap between then and his death, his name was mentioned in a case at Leeds crown court when he was named as the leader of a pornography network.

As police enquiries went on into the ring they learnt that Dr John regularly talked about the way that Bernard had been cut up and boasted of how – while working on the liners – he had killed and cut up a cabin boy after sex. He was obviously a man to be interviewed when he was brought back to England. He could tell about Dr 'X' as well. Both men were tall, handsome and attractive to men and youths.

But Dr John decided he was not going to go down that path and rather than face jail and ruin he booked into the hotel, had a good dinner and a drink in the bar before going up to his room and putting the 'Do not disturb' sign on the door.

He then sat down and wrote three letters, one to his mother, one to a doctor friend and one to Scotland Yard. Then he took an overdose and died.

His death did not solve the mystery for in his letter to Scotland Yard he said that he was sorry for what he had done without going into detail. Whether this was an apology for the murder of Bernard or whether it was to do with the porn ring where he had been described in court as 'an evil man', no one knows and he took that to the grave with him.

Two years later Dr 'X' went to jail in Australia, opening up another enquiry but once more without success. He was saying nothing.

It was the last lead that police followed. The file is still open and if Dr 'X' should reach his death bed and, if the killer wants to make a confession, the file could perhaps be closed. It is reasonable to assume that from all the evidence that the police amassed more than one person took part in the killing of the backward boy. There may have been two or three or even more at the party where he died and that the person who was actually responsible was not one of the doctors who took the body to carve it up in the privacy of their surgery.

It is as strange a mystery as any you can name.

17   Johnson

Champagne Charlie, the Supreme Conman

The lilt of the waltz and the glow from the champagne she had consumed brought an extra sparkle to Kathy's Irish eyes as she smiled at her handsome fiancé. She could not believe her luck. Just a few weeks before she had been appointed his secretary to help him write a book about his life, because it had been so rich and successful. He had been governor of the Bahamas and was now helping the Secret Service to track down spies who were operating in the Galway Bay area.

And here they were now, at the ball of the season, the Waterford Hunt at Lismore Castle, she soon to become Lady Murphy, wife of Colonel Sir Patrick Murphy, war hero, spy catcher, huntsman, patron of the arts. He was a fine figure of a man in his tails, his decorations for bravery on his lapel, his black hair swept back, his cavalry moustache trimmed to perfection, his horn-rimmed glasses adding a further touch of distinction.

They danced to the music and talked of love and their future.

The idyllic moment, which Kathy could still not believe, was being televised by the BBC, so important a social occasion it was. Anyone who was anyone in Eire was there. The hunting crowd, the horsey crowd, the social set, the rich and famous. In those days (1956) the BBC covered such occasions live.

The programme was shown not just in Ireland but also on mainland Britain and among those watching was a detective sergeant in the Metropolitan police. He was at home in London with his wife, idly viewing as he had a glass of beer.

The camera panned across the dancers, naming them for the viewers. 'And there,' intoned the commentator 'is Colonel Sir Patrick Murphy, former governor of the Bahamas and soon to become a Master of the Hunt in this area, with his lovely fiancée, Katherine ...'

The detective leapt from his seat. 'That's not Sir Patrick anyone,' he shouted to his wife. 'That's Champagne Charlie,' and he headed for the phone.

Champagne Charlie was a wanted man. He was always a wanted man when he came out of prison because he could not resist the urge to obtain money from gullible girls and wealthy ladies with tales of his past, his present – which was usually spy hunting for the Secret Service – and his future, which always included them as his wife.

His problem was that having obtained the money he tended to spend it all, and ended up drinking champagne which he had not paid for. It was a path very much followed by Vivian Kenway, played by Rex Harrison in the film *The Rake's Progress*. His best friend toasted him after his death at German hands in the war, standing by his body in a wine store saying, 'Good old Viv, died as he lived, drinking champagne he had not paid for.'

Champagne Charlie's life ran on similar lines but for different reasons. He was army and title mad, a snob who hated reality, for it reminded him just who and what he was, which was a nobody.

His final exploit brought him to Cambridge and ended in violence and death but to understand why, it is necessary to go back to the start of his life.

He was born in 1921, Patrick Johnson, the son of an army officer serving in Burma at the time. His father died before he was born and he was brought up by an uncle who was also an Indian Army officer.

He went to two public schools in the Midlands, both establishments where fagging and flogging were the rule of the day but they did nothing for Charlie who was immune to the hardest beating and severest discipline. He was expelled from both because they realized they could do nothing with him. He had already developed a taste for obtaining property (and taxi rides) without paying for them. He had only one passion and that was for the army. He longed to emulate his father and studied the histories of every regiment in the British army. He knew the traditions and the mess etiquette of all of them. He could answer any question, point to every flag and battle honour and recite the heroes and colonels. But as his educational skills were poor he could not go to Sandhurst to become an officer.

The start of the Second World War in 1939 saw him at Woolwich where he enlisted as Gunner Johnson, Patrick, no. 889648. It was not the sort of title that a fine young soldier wanted. He was in need of promotion and as the army would not do it, he did it himself. The new young subaltern celebrated his commission at the Savoy, inviting MPs, showbiz stars, bankers and fellow officers. Second Lieutenant Sir Patrick Johnson, nineteen-year-old son of Lord Manchester, was in his element as he mixed wth the swells who were only too happy to toast his commission with champagne which their host was paying for.

But of course he was not. The bill was for £300 and for the first, but most certainly not the last time, it was not paid and the host vanished. Not for long however because young Patrick could not resist uniforms and being the centre of attention, with a poppet on his arm (or both arms). The police found him.

Instead of Dunkirk and the desert, the young ex-soldier spent three years in borstal, honing up his training not to be a warrior but a supreme conman. There was no doubting his skill in depriving people of their money and spending it but he never learnt when to stop.

Where he picked up the idea of being a super-spy attached to MI5 no one knows but it was the extra polish to his normal plan of being a very important person with a brilliant past which included a war record that had brought him many medals.

When he came out of Borstal he became Captain George Johnson of MI5 and met a wealthy widow whom he charmed. He convinced her that he was in a key position in the Secret Service because he looked younger than he was and that he was hunting for Rudolph Hess who had managed to escape from captivity. Hess, Hitler's deputy, flew to England soon after war broke out to try and negotiate a peace, an idea which no one took seriously. He stayed in captivity, until he died a very old man in the late eighties. However the dashing captain with a dazzling moustache and a line in patter that charmed ladies into bed as well as out of their money, convinced the widow that Hess was on the run and he was in hot pursuit. He knew the area in which he was hiding but could not locate the exact house. He discovered, he said, that Hess was waiting for a boat to take him out of England. When the widow asked why this was not being made public the 'spycatcher' laughed. Things like this were hush-hush, he said. The public were never told this sort of information.

They stayed in Liverpool and in between bouts in bed and the bar Johnson was out 'Hess hunting'. He came back with exciting news. A Belgian double agent knew exactly where Hess was and the boat on which he was to be smuggled to a neutral country. He wanted £5,000 for the information and Johnson had contacted his office. But there was a snag. It would take two days to get the money to him in Liverpool as it was wartime.

The boat was going the next day and the Belgian would not give the information until he had the money. Could the widow help with a temporary loan? She could. She was infatuated with him and she and he went to the bank and withdrew the money in cash, which was a huge sum in 1943. She handed it to her handsome lover and off he went to pay the Belgian. She never saw him again.

Charlie was not so lucky when he met a student and convinced him that he was hunting Hess – still. It was the same old story and the student almost fell for it but not quite. There was something he did not like about this glib chap who was so smooth and knew so much. Perhaps it was because he talked just that bit too much for someone who was in the Secret Service, but whatever it was the student went to the police. They were waiting in the wings when the spycatcher came to take his winnings from the student and Charlie had his first taste of prison.

It was the first of many visits. The sentences grew longer for in those days there was a form of imprisonment called preventive detention which was geared to keep persistent criminals off the streets for long periods of time by giving them swingeing terms inside with very little remission however well they behaved themselves. Petty thieves who stole from doorsteps suddenly found themselves locked up in Dartmoor for ten years PD with the likes of Champagne Charlie who had several terms of it. He at least brightened some of the long days because so immersed was he in his various roles that he actually convinced one governor that he had been in MI5 and lectured the prisoners on the subject. Outside he was variously a spy, an ex-Japanese PoW, army and RAF officer, master of several hunts and racehorse owner. He was none of these but he was so convincing that he even fooled people into believing that he had only been in prison because he had been caught while working for MI5 – 'if you get caught the department does not want to know you, you just have to serve your time' – he would say. He also managed to talk his way onto top secret army and RAF bases for the sheer hell of it.

One of his best exploits was when he came out after a lengthy sentence in late 1955. He took a lady friend's jewellery and left for Ireland, leaving a fiancée in England

– and more of her shortly – where he met up with Kathy in Eire. It was wonderful at first as he took her everywhere, the people of Ireland taking his word for his background as governor of the Bahamas and no one checking the references he handed out because he looked so real. He became part of the social scene. But what worried Kathy increasingly were his claims that he was an international spy and the danger he was in. It did not click. Again he was overdoing it, and at the same time that the London detective spotted him on television at the hunt ball, Kathy's mother was checking the references that he had given her daughter when he employed her. They were bogus.

He was arrested and brought back to London to be charged over a £585 diamond clip he had persuaded a jeweller to hand to him.

When police investigated what else he had been up to they found Helen, an English rose to whom Charlie – as Major Michael Woodfall, MC, of the Royal Horse Artillery – had proposed marriage. She thought he was the finest type of English gentleman and distinguished army officer so it came as quite a shock when she discovered who and what he really was.

She met him on the steps of the Cavalry Club for an interview as his personal secretary. Within minutes he had told her his life story – prisoner of the Japanese, dropped ito France to organize the Maquis, awarded the MC, just out of the army – and engaged her as his personal secretary to help sort out his affairs and help run the hotel in Cornwall of which he was managing director.

He mentioned friends, all titled or famous, and swept her off her feet. Within thirty hours he was proposing to her and when she explained that she was already married but separated, he said her wedding did not count to the Catholics – and he was a devout one – because it had been in a registry office.

Once down in Cornwall there was not a spare moment.

During the day there were letters and meetings, at night, parties where champagne flowed like water. The social whirl really got going when Charlie heard that the local hunt was short of money and he wrote them a cheque for £100. This took him into the heart of local society and he was riding to hound on his own horse, resplendent in hunting clothes and dancing the night away in tails with his MC ribbon for all to see.

The couple, for Helen considered herself officially engaged even though he did not buy her a ring (although he did buy her a Siamese cat called Sooty to be company for her poodle), stayed at top London hotels and went to the top night spots. He even took her father to the Cavalry Club and behaved like the perfect member which he definitely was not. But such was his manner that he was accepted by the club members and servants.

But as ever he overdid it. He had Helen flashing 'V' signals with a torch from the cliff tops and she began to doubt him. She made the mistake of telling him that she did not believe his 'MI5 theatricals' and it was the wrong thing to do. He sulked like a little boy who had had his belief in Father Christmas taken away.

Two days later over his favourite lunch of oysters, smoked salmon and steak, washed down with wine and loads of champagne, he ordered the girls in the party to go and find dresses for a regimental ball to which he was taking them. At the ball he would introduce them all to the Queen.

There was no ball, no Queen, no Charlie. The man disappeared to Ireland and it was there he was finally caught, brought back, tried and sentenced to nine years' preventive detention. The girls told their stories and he told his but to a different audience on freezing foggy nights in the recreation area of Dartmoor.

His imprisonment did not affect him at all. He had been befriended by a wealthy lady who was a member of the peerage. She invited him to her stately home the day he was released. He arrived and within minutes was behaving to the manner born, complaining about the service that the butler provided.

He also signed up with a marriage agency which led him to Cambridge and the wealthy widow, Effie, five years his senior.

It was love almost at first sight for her. She was lonely after the death of her husband, a businessman, and this handsome military man, Major Michael Patrick Murphy Woodfall, retired recently from the Royal Horse Artillery, seemed the answer to her loneliness. He was soon telling her over a champagne and oyster supper that he owned two hotels in Cornwall and a castle in Ireland (for Charlie never changed the patter) and that he had an income of £30,000 a year topped up with a further £17,000 a year as a beneficiary under a trust. In 1963, £47,000 a year was a very tidy sum. But it was not just that. Dark haired, attractive Effie was impressed by his manner and presence. He had the bearing of a military man with cavalry twills and tweed sports jacket, his fine cut suits, his bristling moustache, the penetrating eyes that stared directly at you and seemed so sincere and convincing.

She took him home and within three weeks they were so in love – she genuinely, oh so genuinely, and he so insincerely, oh so insincerely – that he proposed marriage and she, poor sweet innocent woman, accepted.

He forgot to tell her two crucial things – that, he was already married and that he did not have a penny in the world.

He soon saw to the latter, borrowing over £2,000 in the days after their wedding on 29 April and topped it up as they went along on a spree of high living throughout the summer.

When they were in Cambridge he could be seen propping up the bar in the main hotels with the adoring Effie at his side or holding forth in a wine bar where many of the dons called in for a drink on King's Parade. He had stories that he could tell in such a way that he held his audience. Effie was thrilled. She did not mind lending him the money because he gave her a £20,000 cheque in trust but asked her not to cash it for the time being because accountants were sorting out some affairs on his estates and castle in Eire. He told her that he would settle £17,000 on her daughter when she became twenty-one in four years' time, and that a joint bank account would make sense. Effie agreed.

They went to the Continent and Charlie explained that he had to look at some horses for he sometimes worked for the British Bloodstock Agency. Then they returned before going to Ireland for the summer. They travelled in style, for he hired a Silver Cloud Rolls-Royce and a chauffeur for £88 a week, and it was he who drove them to the family home, the ancestral home of his family the Woodfalls, Bermingham House in Co. Galway.

He told his adoring bride that Lady Cusack-Smith had lived there for twenty years as his housekeeper but he was now coming home to take his place at the head of the family. For, surprise, surprise, not least to the impressed bride, he was really Sir Patrick Murphy Woodfall and he had given up his title because his mother had taken a vow of poverty. She believed him.

The truth was that he had never seen the place before in his life. He had no notion that there was an enormous fireplace in the house which he called Gort Castle in front of which his mother – and he once pulled up outside a peasant's cottage and rushed in and out and said that that was his mother's home and that he always stopped to give her a kiss because she shunned meeting people because of her vow – had dangled him as a child. He was in fact renting it from Mrs Cusack-Smith for £60 out of Effie's dwindling money. She was well off before she met Charlie.

They had a marvellous summer, he investing £1000 in the local hunt and becoming joint master, his customary entry into local society as we know. He hired a permanent suite at the Shelbourne Hotel in Dublin for £50 a week, bought bloodstock mares, drank champagne and ate as if it was all going out of fashion.

He and Effie flew back to England regularly and had parties in Cambridge and at the Derby where Charlie won a packet on the last race of the day and celebrated in tremendous style with his own money – for once.

They were back for Ascot and again he overdid it. Effie had invited a couple she knew from the university when her husband said that he had tickets for the Royal Ball at Windsor Castle. The other couple were as excited as Effie and her husband had her practising curtsies ready for the moment when he introduced her to the Queen. This was taking his ploy with his fiancée Helen some nine years before one stage further but Effie had no idea. Why should she? You might wonder why she was taken in, why no one checked on his background, why none of her friends were suspicious, why the local police did not spot him. But why should anyone have been suspicious? He had personality, vitality, money (even if it was not his own) and a presence and talk that was completely convincing. He was also operating in a part of the country where the police did not know him.

So Effie practised the curtsy not knowing that the invitations that her husband flashed around and kept on the mantelpiece were as false as he was.

They went to Ascot, in the Royal Enclosure, where he was as at home as he was on a horse, and everything was going wonderfully well until over the loudspeaker came a message calling for Major Michael Patrick Murphy Woodfall to go to the stewards' office. He excused himself and in his grey top hat and tails hurried away from his wife and guests.

He came back, sad faced and red eyed, with bad news. He had had a telegram to say that his beloved aunt, Lady Pamela Duckworth, had died and in the circumstances, he was so sorry to say, he had to go into mourning as was the family tradition and therefore they would not be going to the ball. It would not be right, the depressed and mournful conman announced. They could go on enjoying the races but he would wait in the Rolls.

It was – of course – Charlie who had sent the telegram himself, a master stroke by a master confidence trickster, to get himself out of a very tricky situation where exposure was inevitable.

It was only delaying the day. A friend of Effie's became suspicious. Everything seemed just too right about the retired major until he made a slight mistake about his regiment. It was not a big one but a mistake that a real major who had spent his life in the regiment, the Royal Horse Artillery, would have known. The friend had a friend in the CID and asked him casually as friends can do, if anything was known about this energetic, fast spending, smooth talking man who had made a mistake about an important date in the regiment's recent history? Had he ever come to the notice of the police, for he did not seem quite real? A check was made and the police knew just who the major was. But he did not appear to have done anything serious. Certainly his wife had made no complaint. A detective went to see Charlie and during the interview the conman admitted that he had lied to the registrar when saying that he was not married but of course he had no idea of the whereabouts of his first wife and yes, it was true that he was not a major.

Effie was told. She was very upset but he used every ounce of the skill he had acquired as a supreme liar to convince her that he had to behave in this way because he was working for MI5. He had been a spycatcher for them for years, repeating the story he had used before, but adding extra details such as the fact that he had been a prisoner of the Germans and becaues of his work they had put him into several camps including Belsen where they had burnt his face with matches. He showed her the scars hidden behind his moustache to prove that he had been in the hands of the torturers in the concentration camp.

She was convinced. He then played his master card. He told her that as part of his work for the intelligence service he had had to go to jail to catch an enemy agent – so important that sacrificing almost a decade of his life was worth it for serving one's country. Nine years for a first offence, a non-existent crime invented by his masters, was almost unbelievable but such was his spell on Effie that she was convinced – for a while.

But the magic was beginning to wear off. She was noticing little things that she had not bothered to notice before or probably were not there. If you do not know, there is nothing to watch out for. But when you do know that your husband has married you bigamously, was not a major and had spent nine years in prison, then a little niggle is bound to appear at the back of your brain. The relationship is spoilt. I can understand how it happens because (and this is nothing to do with crime!) I had always been a tremendous fan of Tony Hancock and used to find his stares were a magical addition to his skills. But then I saw a programme about his life and his producer said that in 'The Blood Donor', a classic of comedy, the stares were not because of humour but because he was reading his lines as he was too lazy to learn them. I can no longer watch him because I know what he is doing and it is spoilt forever. I imagine that Charlie had the same effect on Effie as he stood at the bar telling the usual stories of war, his days in the mess, life in the regiment, his heroic tales, his stately home and the lovely Gort Castle which he had given her as a wedding present. Was that really his?

They were staying in a London hotel when the crunch came. Effie never said what was the final straw that sent her back to Cambridge many thousands of pounds poorer but as far as she was concerned it was the end of her marriage and relationship with Champagne Charlie.

But for once he would not let go. He tried attempted

suicide when she refused to see him. He called but she refused to answer the door, or the phone and she refused to accept the bunches of flowers and the red roses he sent her.

She knew that if she did, he would start talking, would cast his spell and she might be tempted to have him back, even knowing his appalling record and just what he was.

So Charlie turned to the one crime he had never before committed: violence.

He hired two local thugs, pretending he was working for a Sunday newspaper and that he was covering a matrimonial dispute in which the wife was playing hard to get while her husband waited for a reunion. They drove to Effie's home in a village just outside Cambridge.

For the first time in his life he used a shotgun instead of his tongue to grab his victim. He walked into the house and at a gunpoint pushed Effie outside. She screamed and screamed but the quick-witted conman was ready for that.

As the neighbours poured out of their houses, the gun and Effie were hurled into the car where the youths grabbed her arms. Charlie shouted, 'It's all right. Don't worry, I'm a doctor, and I'm taking her to hospital for her own good. She's had a collapse.'

Off into the night the car roared. The neighbours were not all convinced and the police were rung. Effie lay on the back seat with sticking plaster over her mouth, scared out of her wits. Any feeling she had for her 'husband' went in that moment.

And as she lay there shaking, the police spotted the car and began to chase at speeds up to 100 mph. At a roadblock fifteen miles from Cambridge, Charlie kept going and knocked a policeman off his motorcycle and disappeared into the night.

It was too much for the yobs, big mouthed louts who would offer violence at the bang of a bar glass. They did not like being in a car travelling at over 100 miles an hour with the driver armed with a gun and a kidnapped woman lying on the back seat. They wanted out and pleaded with Charlie to stop. He did and with words that said clearly what he thought about their yellow-bellied behaviour, put them out into the night. But not Effie.

He drove on until he turned into a farm track where he stopped to take some pills washed down with whisky. Effie took her life into her hands, kicked the car door open and ran for it in the pouring rain. As she ran she slipped and then fell into a ditch. She dragged herself out and made her way to the road where she flagged down a passing motorist. In her bedraggled state she told her story and he drove her to a phone where she rang the police.

They found Charlie soon after. Like the woman he professed to love he had fallen in a ditch.

That should have been the end. Normally the criminal, as we know, appears before a court, is sent for trial and then sentenced and taken to prison.

With Charlie it was not like that. Why should anyone be surprised?

He was charged with obtaining a total of £4,400 from Effie by false pretences.

The second time he appeared before Cambridge magistrates to be remanded in custody until his committal proceedings, he was brought from Bedford prison, handcuffed with a prison officer as escort, in a taxi. The old Cambridge police station had a large well in the centre in which cars and police and prison vans could park. The taxi pulled into the well and Charlie was first out, his umbrella over his arm. As his escort moved to follow him Charlie said that he had forgotten his papers and could the officer please get them.

In the second or so as the escort instinctively turned, Charlie was gone – through the door of the well, through the front door and out into the streets, packed with shoppers, students and cyclists. He ran flat out, his handcuffed hands covered by his umbrella.

He headed for a taxi firm he knew. As he hired a Morris Oxford for the day he struggled under his umbrella and managed to get the handcuffs off. He had very small hands and he was very practised at such arts.

Then he told the driver, John, what he wanted. First they would go to Newmarket, then to Royston, then to London and then back to Cambridge late afternoon when he would pay.

Newmarket? To the Subscription Rooms to obtain three entry forms to enter horses he did not own nor existed in three races which actually did exist. He was given the forms for who was to doubt the smart little man with bristling moustache and military manner accompanied by cavalry twills and hacking jacket.

Royston? To go and see a well-known trainer to discuss with him Charlie's string of horses and whether the trainer would take them on. Charlie had perfect detail of every fictitious nag and the trainer was impressed.

Then Charlie took the taxi driver to the best hotel in Royston where they lunched on oysters and smoked salmon and beef washed down with lashings of champagne and they departed for London without paying the bill.

He was doing this while a very big search was going on for him. Police had road blocks everywhere. Every available policeman was out looking for the man with the moustache and handcuffs. They could not see how he had got out of Camrbidge. Taxi and car hire firms were checked but no one in handcuffs had hired a car.

By the time they found the firm whose driver had taken Charlie to London he was already on his way there. He stopped for a drink – champagne, what else! – in the bar of the Regent Palace, treating his driver once again. Charlie told him that he had to meet a trainer and a fellow owner and then they would head back to Cambridge. He would not be a minute, he said, but he had to go to the gents. The driver sat finishing his drink and waiting. He waited a long time before he realized that his fare was not coming back.

Charlie had gone out the back entrance of the hotel and vanished again without paying the bill. He left that to the driver from whom he had borrowed money until he could get to the bank. It is easy to understand why he would do anything to escape. It was not just the five charges of false pretences he faced but far more seriously, possessing a shotgun at the time he maliciously wounded Effie. On the conman charges he faced at least a twelve year imprisonment but with the wounding on top of it and the vicious, cowardly way he did it, he could get another five or six years. He was forty-two and with full remission he would be well into his fifties when he came out. It was not an encouraging prospect.

He headed for Paddington with its hundreds of hotels and booked into one for the night while he considered what to do next and where to go to do it. The hotel was comfortable with a bar and dining-room, just the place to stay with other anonymous people spending a night or two in London on business or pleasure, a place where there might be a gullible woman on whom he could work his magic.

But of all the hundreds he had to pick, he chose the wrong one. It was run by a woman who had run a hotel in Westport, Co. Mayo, eight years before, when Charlie was having his Irish fling with the lovely Kathy. The woman recognized her new guest, Peter Mitchell, even though now he had a fiery moustache which he was not wearing the last time she saw him. She rang the police.

As he came down for breakfast the men from the Yard arrived and escorted the protesting guest outside. They went down the steps to the street where people were hurrying to the underground to go to work. Suddenly Charlie shouted out, 'In the name of the Queen, help me arrest these people. They are criminals.'

The passers-by stopped as the three men struggled on

the steps with Charlie still calling for help. The police were shouting that they were police and as some of the crowd moved to his aid, one of the detectives swore loudly at the outrageous stroke this old conman had pulled.

'There,' roared Charlie, 'I told you. Policeman wouldn't swear like that,' and the crowd debagged one of the policemen as the struggle went on. It ended when one produced both his warrant card which he waved to the crowd, and handcuffs which he managed to get on Charlie, whom he also had in an armlock.

He was taken back to Cambridge and then to Bedford prison where he waited two months, spending Christmas there, until his trial in mid-January 1964, at Norwich in the assizes court.

Effie went to see him, to hear what he had done, to hear his past and most of all to hear what he would say – what lies he would tell and how he would explain it all.

Patrick Johnson pleaded not guilty to all the charges and listened as the familiar story was outlined to the jury. Then Effie gave evidence, slowly and sadly, occasionally glancing over to the man in the dock whose eyes rarely left her. He had a penetrating stare and you could see how it could mesmerize women.

Then it was his turn. It was a sorry sight. He told a good story, about being blackmailed by an ex-prisoner, days in prison for the MI5, all the flights of fancy that had fooled the rich, the VIPs, MPs, lords and ladies, social sets in Eire and London, but suddenly it had no conviction. He was asked late in the afternoon as Effie sat in the public gallery listening, if his story did not have a familiar ring about it, for was it not very much like the one he had told eight years earlier when he was last convicted? He fumbled a few words and said yes, they probably were, but they were true.

Then as darkness fell outside and the lights of the streets flickered in the windows, there was silence. It was clear, very clear, that no one believed him. There was no need for the prosecuting counsel who was cross-examining him to ask anything else. Anything more that Charlie's glib tongue said was worthless.

He was an empty shell out of which all spirit had gone as he was led back to the dock for the last time. The next morning there would be closing speeches and the judge would sum up, but everyone in the court knew it was a foregone conclusion and no one would take much time to do their jobs.

The judge rose and they took Charlie down the steps. The sparkle of champagne had gone. He was as flat as last year's bottle.

Effie sat in the back of the court for a long time. Then she too left, planning to return the next day for the finish.

It was not to be. The officers at Norwich jail had been warned that he might do something desperate. He had attempted suicide three times after Effie had left him but they were not very serious attempts. He had always been found and the pills pumped out. But this time, to make sure that nothing happened in the night, his cell was searched. The mirror taken out, any of his clothing that could be used to hang himself was removed, and a nail and a needle were pulled out of the wall. The cell light was left on and a check made every fifteen minutes.

But Champagne Charlie had spent twenty of the last twenty-five years of his life in jail and knew every trick in the book, including how to smuggle something into his cell past the most vigilant search.

He had hidden a sliver of razor blade, no more than quarter of an inch long. With it he cut the two main veins in his left arm and under the blanket he quietly bled to death in the way that an officer and a gentleman, the two things he so longed to be, the two things he played so well, might go.

It was just after five o'clock when an officer spotted through the peep hole the trickle of blood seeping down the blanket and on to the floor. But it was too late. He was dead.

Effie arrived at the court just before the starting time of 10.30 and the first she knew was when the detective in charge of the case, who had brought her the sixty miles from Cambridge because she was the main prosecution witness, told her. She insisted on being in court while the judge was told and the jury was dismissed. No one brings in a verdict on a dead defendant.

She sat at the back of the court on her own for a very long time after everyone had gone. Then she came outside and was quite happy to talk briefly about him.

She had said when she first gave evidence at Cambridge magistrates court that she had wanted to wait until the autumn to marry when he first proposed in their whirlwind courtship but, 'he said he needed me and that he was rather lonely and I rather understood that point of view because I was rather the same. So I agreed to marry him sooner.'

What did she feel now? She smiled her slow smile and picking her words, she said, 'I pity him. But this was the ultimate end for this man because of the life he led. It was the only way to end it. I had no feeling left for him. Naturally I am upset. It was a shock, of course it was. His lies were so convincing. I never dreamt of disbelieving him. Even when he told me he had just served nine years in prison, for his first-ever crime, I still never thought of disbelieving him.'

Then she said, 'But I don't reproach myself at all. I don't think I am to blame. It was the only way.'

A few days later Patrick Johnson was buried in a pauper's grave in Norwich cemetery. There was no tombstone to remind people that Champagne Charlie lay there. There was only one bunch of flowers and that caused a story in one of the Sunday papers that speculated it came from one of the women whose heart he had broken.

It did not. An old Cambridge journalist colleague Michael Jeacock and I sent it. Perhaps it was a silly thing to do but despite his wicked audacious ways he had a touch of class that amused and fascinated people and us. He could not go without some appreciation.

Index